Railways Restored

Guide to preserved railways, steam centres and railway museums

1984/85 edition

LONDON
IAN ALLAN LTD

First published 1984

ISBN 0 7110 1372 1

Published by Ian Allan Ltd, Shepperton, Surrey; and printed by Ian Allan Printing Ltd at their works at Coombelands in Runnymede, England

The publishers, the railway operators and the Association of Railway Preservation Societies accept no liability for any loss, damage or injury caused by error or inaccuracy in the information published in *Railways Restored 1984/5. Train services may be altered or cancelled without prior notice, and at some locations diesel traction may be substituted for scheduled steam workings.*

Contents

The colour pages in this edition take a look at some of the aspects of railway preservation over the last 25 years.

Cover:
Former LNER 'Y7' class 0-4-0T No 68088 in action at Loughborough, Great Central Railway, 22 October 1983.
J. H. Cooper-Smith

Title page:
Main line steam at Garsdale. SR 4-6-0 No 777 *Sir Lamiel* heads the 'Cumbrian Mountain Pullman' on 4 December 1982. *L. A. Nixon*

Left:
No 3205 seen leaving Bridgnorth with a SVR train in September 1982. *T. Grimshaw*

The numbers on the map refer to the page the entry appears on.

25 Years of Railway Preservation
The Silver Jubilee of the ARPS

The idea of a National Association of Railway Preservation Societies was the brainchild of Noel Draycott and the first recorded meeting took place on 21 November 1959 at the Station Hotel Stafford.

This inaugural meeting, at which Noel Draycott acted as General Secretary, laid the foundation of the West Midland District of the Railway Preservation Society and launched the national campaign.

Noel Draycott campaigned for a National Council to cover the country. Terry Kirtland and his magazine *Forum* ('Magazine of the Railway Preservation Societies') was in at the start and gave good publicity cover to the campaign.

Over the next few years the enthusiasm from the West Midlands Group spread and affiliations included The Scottish RPS — The London RPS — The Keighley and Worth Valley RPS — The Princess Elizabeth Society — The Dowty RPS and the Middleton Railway Trust. All are flourishing to-day and the Middleton became the first standard gauge preserved railway.

Simultaneously down south Noel Draycott attended the foundation meeting of the Bluebell Railway held at Haywards Heath in March 1959. Bluebell became the second standard gauge railway and the first to carry passengers.

1959 thus saw the start of standard gauge preservation and the formation of a united 'umbrella' for all preservation societies.

After many birth pangs the National Council of the Railway Preservation Society grew into the Association of Railway Preservation Societies with David Ives as Chairman, Roger Bell General Secretary, Ken Vincent Minutes Secretary, Bob Yates Treasurer, Terry Kirtland Editor of Forum and Peter Manisty Publicity Officer.

Sadly Noel Draycott died on 22 November 1967 and did not see his dream finally fulfilled. His name is perpetuated in the ARPS Noel Draycott Memorial award in the ARPS Magazine competition.

The ARPS now contains over 90% of the voluntary movement and has 134 railway preservation societies in its membership together with many private members.

The original aims remain 'To further the mutual co-operation of railway preservation groups, to promote publicity on their behalf and to encourage high standards of competence and safety'.

A pictorial survey of the first 25 years is contained in this Silver Jubilee edition of our Yearbook *Railways Restored*.

Be sure and join the ARPS as a Private Member and take part in our Jubilee celebrations (see page 93).

Over the years the ARPS has built up a very close liaison with other bodies concerned with railway preservation — in particular — The Department of Transport (whose Inspecting Officers of Railways are closely associated with our railways). The Transport Trust (who take care of fund-raising). British Rail, The Association of Minor Railway Companies (AMRC) and the Science Museum and its satellite the National Railway Museum.

Dame Margaret Weston DBE the Director of the Science Museum is President of the Association.

The dates and locations for 1984/5 meetings is as follows:

Saturday/Sunday, 19/20 May
Keighley & Worth Valley Railway
Saturday/Sunday, 29/30 September
North Norfolk Railway
Saturday/Sunday, 26/27 January 1985
Annual General Meeting, York

Peter Manisty MBE
Captain, RN (Retd)

Sheringham Station,
Norfolk, NR26 8RA

ARPS Annual Award

This is made to a member Group making an outstanding contribution to voluntary railway preservation during the year of the Award.

Previous awards have been made to:

1975—the Great Western Society Ltd
1976—the Princess Elizabeth Locomotive Society
1977—the Peterborough Railway Society Ltd (Nene Valley Railway)
1978—the Festiniog Railway Society
1979—the Severn Valley Railway Co Ltd
1980—the Scottish Railway Preservation Society Co Ltd
1981—the Great Western Society Ltd
1982—The Festiniog Railway Society Ltd

The ARPS Annual Award

The Association of Railway Preservation Societies Ltd annual award for 1983 is made to the Railway Preservation Society of Ireland for its continuing highly successful operation during 1983 — as for many years past — of steam excursions, comprised of its own locomotives and coaches over the lines of both Coras Iompair Eireann and Northern Ireland Railways, together with the restoration to traffic during the year of LMS (NCC) 2-6-4T locomotive No 4 (after a five year overhaul), UTA dining car No 87, GSWR coach No 1142 and LMS (NCC) coach No 91.

Preserved Railways and Preservation Centres

Editorial

The editor would like to congratulate the Assocation of Railway Preservation Societies on reaching its silver jubilee. Railway preservation has come a long way in the last 25 years and the colour pages of this edition of *Railways Restored* show only a fraction of what individuals and societies have achieved during that period.

Much time and effort have gone into restoring the epitomy of railways — the steam locomotive — to its rightful place, often to the exclusion of other times, although of just as much importance. 1984 has therefore been designated as the 'Year of the Coach'. Various societies have restored pre-nationalisation, and even pre-grouping, vehicles to their former glory but a large percentage of lines rely on life-expired British Rail Mark 1 vehicles — often with just a coat of paint to disguise their former ownership.

For many non-enthusiast visitors the ride is more imortant than the shine on the locomotive — should they have to put up with the same conditions that they get from BR?

Another side of railway preservation that has seemed to be the poor relation is that of diesels, they are after all part of our railway heritage, and *now* is the time to act, too much has already been lost.

The National Railway Museum has acquired the former York diesel depot, would it be too much to hope that it will become the part of the museum showing the diesel era, while the current building is restricted to that of the steam era — the contrast between what we have, and had, would be quite marked. Alternatively should a BR diesel depot close, Southall has been ear-marked, the opportunity for creating a centre for diesel preservation should not be missed.

Alan Butcher

Editor's Notes

On the following pages will be found a guide to the major preserved railways, railway museums and preservation centres in the British Isles. Information for visitors has been set out in tabular form for easy reference, together with a complete locomotive stocklist for each centre. The geographical location of each line or centre is indicated on the map on page 4 by the appropriate page number.

Many preservation centres and operating lines provide facilities for other groups and organisations to restore locomotives and equipment on their premises. It has not been possible to include full details of these groups, but organisations which own locomotives are shown under the centres at which they operate. In addition a full list of member societies of the ARPS is given on page 90. In the case of most operating lines their length is given but there is no guarantee that services are operated over the entire length.

Under the heading **References** will be found the details of articles which have appeared in the Ian Allan magazines: *Railway World* and *Trains Illustrated* during the past two years.

Abbreviations

AEC	Associated Equipment Company	O&K	Orenstein & Koppel
A/Barclay	Andrew Barclay & Sons	RSH	Robert Stephenson & Hawthorn Ltd
A/Porter	Aveling & Porter Ltd	R/Hornsby	Ruston Hornsby
A/Whitworth	Armstrong Whitworth	R/Proctor	Ruston Proctor
B/Peacock	Beyer Peacock & Co	YEC	Yorkshire Engine Co
B/Hawthorn	Black, Hawthorn & Co	BE	Battery electric
BTH	British Thomson Houston	DE	Diesel-electric
D/Metcalfe	Davies & Metcalfe	DH	Diesel-hydraulic
E/Electric	English Electric Ltd	DM	Diesel-mechanical
F/Jennings	Fletcher Jennings & Co	E	Overhead electric
F/Walker	Fox Walker	F	Fireless
G/England	George England & Co	G	Geared
H/Clarke	Hudswell Clarke & Co Ltd	PM	Petrol-mechanical
H/Leslie	Hawthorn Leslie & Co	ParM	Paraffin mechanical
K/Stuart	Kerr Stuart & Co Ltd	PT	Pannier tank
M/Rail	Motor Rail Ltd	R	Railcar
M/Vick	Metrovick (Metropolitan-Vickers)	ST	Saddle tank
M/Wardle	Manning Wardle & Co Ltd	T	Side tanks
N/British	North British Locomotive Co Ltd	VB	Vertical boiler
N/Wilson	Nasmyth Wilson & Co Ltd	4w	4-wheel

SOUTH-EAST

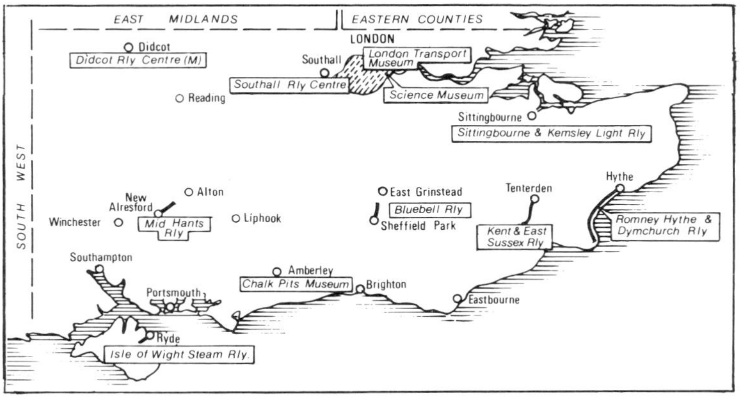

Bluebell Railway

Headquarters: Bluebell Railway Preservation Society, Sheffield Park station, Uckfield, East Sussex TN22 3QL
Telephone: Newick 2370
Main station: Sheffield Park
Other public stations: Horsted Keynes
Car parks: Sheffield Park, Horsted Keynes
Access by public transport: Haywards Heath BR and bus to Horsted Keynes village weekdays, or direct to Sheffield Park in summer and winter Sundays. Additional bus services on certain days, timetable brochure available by sending sae
Refreshment facilities: Sheffield Park, Horsted Keynes
Souvenir shops: Sheffield Park, Horsted Keynes
Museum: Sheffield Park
Depots: Sheffield Park (locomotives), Horsted Keynes (stock)
Passenger trains: Sheffield Park-Horsted Keynes (5 miles)
Period of public operation: Sundays in January, February and December, also Boxing and New Year's Day. Saturdays and Sundays in March, April and November. Wednesdays, Saturdays and Sundays in May and October. Daily June-September inclusive. Open for limited viewing at other times
Facilities for disabled: All station facilities are on the level and ramps available for placing wheelchair visitors into trains
Special notes: Vintage and special weekends are held during the year
Feature article references: RW November 1982 p586 (photo feature); RW August 1983 p401; TI No 43 p23; TI No 44 p24.

Locomotives

Name	*No*	*Origin*	*Class*	*Type*	*Built*
—	27	SECR	P	0-6-0T	1910
Stepney	55	LBSCR	A1X	0-6-0T	1875
Fenchurch	72	LBSCR	A1X	0-6-0T	1872
Pioneer II	178	SECR	P	0-6-0T	1910
*Bluebell**	323	SECR	P	0-6-0T	1910
—	263	SECR	H	0-4-4T	1905
Birch Grove	473	LBSCR	E4	0-6-2T	1898
—	30583	LSWR	0415	4-4-2T	1885
—	592	SECR	C	0-6-0	1901
—	2650	NLR		0-6-0T	1880
Earl of Berkeley	3217	GWR	9000	4-4-0	1938
—	30064	SR	USA	0-6-0T	1943
—	33001	SR	Q1	0-6-0	1942
—	541	SR	Q	0-6-0	1939
—	30847	SR	S15	4-6-0	1937
Stowe	928	SR	V	4-4-0	1934
—	1618	SR	U	2-6-0	1928
—	31638	SR	U	2-6-0	1931
—	30096	LSWR	B4	0-4-0T	1905

BR Class 4MT No 75027 arriving at Horsted Keynes, April 1983. *A. C. Butcher*

Name	No	Origin	Class	Type	Built
Sir Archibald Sinclair	34059	SR	BB	4-6-2	1947
Camelot	73082	BR	5MT	4-6-0	1955
—	75027	BR	4MT	4-6-0	1954
—	78059†	BR	2MT	2-6-0	1956
—	80100	BR	4MT	2-6-4T	1954
—	92240	BR	9F	2-10-0	1959
Blackmore Vale	21C123	SR	WC	4-6-2	1946

Industrial locomotives

Name	No	Builder	Type	Built
Blue Circle	—	A/Porter (9449)	2-2-0TG	1926
Baxter	—	F/Jennings (158)	0-4-0T	1877
Stamford	—	Avonside (1972)	0-6-0ST	1927
Sharpthorn	—	M/Wardle	0-6-0ST	1877

*On loan to East Somerset Railway
†Purchased without tender, for conversion to tank engine

Stock
Substantial collection of pre-Nationalisation coaches including SECR, Bulleid, Maunsell and Chesham vehicles. Also freight stock

Owners
592 (the Wainwright C Class Preservation Society)
1618 (the Maunsell Locomotive Society Ltd)
541 (the Maunsell Locomotive Society Ltd)
30847 (the Maunsell Locomotive Society Ltd)
30096 (the Bulleid Society Ltd)
21C123 (the Bulleid Society Ltd)
263 (the H Class Trust)
73082 (the Camelot Locomotive Society)
33001 (on loan from the National Railway Museum)
928 (on loan from Montagu Venturers Ltd)

Isle of Wight Steam Railway

Headquarters: Isle of Wight Steam Railway, Haven Street station, Ryde, Isle of Wight PO33 4DS
Main station: Haven Street
Car park: Haven Street
Access by public transport: Southern Vectis bus services Nos 3/43 from Ryde (connecting with ferries from Portsmouth) and Newport
Refreshment facilities: Light refreshments available
Souvenir shop: Haven Street
Museum: Small exhibits museum at Haven Street
Depot: Haven Street
Passenger trains: Haven Street-Wootton (2 miles)

Locomotives

Name	No	Origin	Class	Type	Built
Freshwater	W8 (32646)	LBSCR	A1X	0-6-0T	1876
—	11 (32640)	LBSCR	A1X	0-6-0T	1878
Calbourne	W24	LSWR	02	0-4-4T	1891

Ex-LBCSR 'Terrier' restored to SR olive green livery as No W8 *Freshwater.*
J. Mackett

Period of public operation: Sundays Easter then May-September. Thursdays July and August. Daily week before August Bank Holiday. Bank Holiday Mondays, Easter, May, Spring, August
Special notes: Island Steam Extravaganza, August Bank Holiday Saturday, Sunday and Monday. Traction Engines, Fairground Organs, Vintage Cars, etc
Feature article reference: TI No 46 p16; TI No 48 p32

Industrial locomotives

Name	No	Builder	Type	Built
Vectis	37	H/Leslie (3135)	0-4-0ST	1915
Ajax	38	Barclay (1605)	0-6-0T	1918
Spitfire	39	R/Hornsby (242868)	4wDM	1946
Tiger	—	N/British (27415)	0-4-0	1954

Stock
3 IWR coaches (bodies only)
3 LBSCR coaches
3 SECR coaches
2 LCDR coaches (bodies only)
1 crane
1 ex-BR ballast tamper
1 Wickham trolley
22 wagons

Kent & East Sussex Railway

Headquarters: Tenterden Railway Co Ltd, Tenterden Town station, Tenterden, Kent TN30 6HE
Telephone: Tenterden 2943
Main station: Tenterden Town
Other public stations: Rolvenden, Wittersham Road
Car parks: Tenterden, Wittersham Road
Access by public transport: Maidstone & District bus service No 400 from Ashford (Kent) BR station
Refreshment facilities: Tenterden Town. Also on train facilities
Souvenir shop: Tenterden Town station
Museum: Station Road, Tenterden
Depot: Rolvenden
Passenger trains: Tenterden-Hexden Bridge. Hourly 11.00-17.00 on Bank Holidays. Otherwise 11.45, 13.45, 15.00 and 16.15 from Tenterden
Period of public operation: Weekends and Bank Holidays from Easter to New Year, plus Wednesdays and Thursdays June and July. Daily throughout August
Facilities for disabled: A special coach for disabled people, 'Petros', is allocated to most trains (telephone for confirmation of availability), reserved parking at Tenterden. Toilets with disabled access at Tenterden, and in coach 'Petros'
Special notes: 'Wealden Pullman' dining car service operates on most Saturday evenings in season. Advance booking is essential for this train. Santa special services operate on each Saturday and Sunday in December. Advanced booking recommended

Owners
10 (London Borough of Sutton)
21 and 22 Kent & East Sussex Loco Trust
14 Resco (Railways) Ltd

Locomotives

Name	No	Origin	Class	Type	Built
Bodiam	3 (32670)	LBSCR	A1X	0-6-0T	1872
Sutton	10 (32650)	LBSCR	A1X	0-6-0T	1876
Pride of Sussex	11 (31556)	SECR	P	0-6-0T	1909
Wainwright	21 (30070)	SR	USA	0-6-0T	1943
Maunsell	22 (30065)	SR	USA	0-6-0T	1943
—	20	GWR	AEC	diesel railcar	1940
—	W79978	BR	AC Cars	diesel railbus	1959
—	19	NSB	21c	2-6-0	1919
—	44 (D2023)	BR	03	0-6-0DM	1958
—	45 (D2024)	BR	03	0-6-0DM	1958
—	46 (D2205)	BR	04	0-6-0DM	1958

Industrial locomotives

Name	No	Builder	Type	Built
Marcia	12	Peckett (1631)	0-4-0T	1923
Charwelton	14	M/Wardle (1955)	0-6-0ST	1917
Rhyl	15	M/Wardle (2009)	0-6-0ST	1921
Dolobran	16	M/Wardle (1762)	0-6-0ST	1910
Arthur	17	M/Wardle (1601)	0-6-0ST	1903
Westminster	18	Peckett (1378)	0-6-0ST	1914
Holman F. Stephens	23	Hunslet (3791)	0-6-0ST	1952
William H. Austen	24	Hunslet (3800)	0-6-0ST	1953
Northiam	25	Hunslet (3797)	0-6-0ST	1953
Linda	26	Hunslet (3781)	0-6-0ST	1952
Rolvenden	27	RSH (7086)	0-6-0ST	1943
—	29	RSH (7667)	0-6-0ST	1950
—	40	BTH	Bo-Bo	1932
Baglan	41	Bagnall (8377)	0-4-0DM	1962
—	42	Hunslet (4208)	0-6-0DM	1948
—	43	Fowler (4220031)	0-4-0DH	1964

Stock
3 ex-SECR 'Birdcage' coaches
1 ex-LSWR coach
3 4-wheel coaches
3 Pullman cars
5 ex-BR Mk1 coaches
1 ex-BR Mk 1 RU 'Diana'
8 ex-SR Maunsell coaches
2 steam cranes
Large interesting collection of freight vehicles

Mid-Hants Railway

Headquarters: Winchester & Alton Railway PLC, Alresford station, Alresford, Hants SO24 9JG
Telephone: Alresford 3810
Main station: Alresford
Other public stations: Ropley, Medstead & Four Marks
Car park: Alresford
Access by public transport: Winchester and Alton BR stations, Alder Valley bus service No 214 (weekdays) and No 453 (Sundays). Telephone Guildford 575226 (Alder Valley) for details
Refreshment facilities: Buffet service on most trains
Souvenir shops: Alresford, Ropley
Depot: Ropley
Passenger trains: Alresford-Medstead & Four Marks. Saturdays, Sundays and bank holidays from 10 March-28 October. Frequent service 11.30-16.50. Daily 23 July-31 August
Length of line: 6 miles
Period of public operation: Weekends and Bank Holidays from mid March-end October
Facilities for disabled: Toilets at Ropley, special facilities for disabled passengers on selected trains
Feature article references: RW January 1982 p35; TI No 44 p9

Locomotives

Name	*No*	*Origin*	*Class*	*Type*	*Built*
—	30120	LSWR	T9	4-4-0	1899
—	30499	LSWR	S15	4-6-0	1920
—	506	LSWR	S15	4-6-0	1920
—	31625	SR	U	2-6-0	1929
—	31806	SR	U	2-6-0	1926
—	31874	SR	N	2-6-0	1925
Bodmin	34016	SR	WC	4-6-2	1945
Tangmere	34067	SR	BB	4-6-2	1947
Swanage	34105	SR	WC	4-6-2	1950
British India Line	35018	SR	MN	4-6-2	1945
—	44123	LMS	4F	0-6-0	1925
—	47324	LMS	3F	0-6-0T	1926
—	76017	BR	4MT	2-6-0	1954

Industrial locomotives

Name	*No*	*Builder*	*Type*	*Built*
—	3	H/Clarke (1544)	0-6-0ST	1924
—	4	Fowler (22889)	0-4-0DM	1939
Errol Lonsdale	196	Hunslet (3796)	0-6-0ST	1953
—	—	N/British (27078)	0-4-0DM	1953

Stock
3 steam cranes
1 'Plassermatic' tamping/levelling machine
1 Plasser & Theurer AL250 lining machine
30 ex-BR Mk1 coaches
10 ex-SR coaches
3 ex-LSWR coaches
1 ex-LMS coach
Numerous goods vehicles

Owners
3 (Slough Estates)
30120 (on loan from the National Railway Museum)
30499 (the Urie S15 Locomotive Preservation Group)
506 (the Urie S15 Locomotive Preservation Group)
34105 (the 34105 Light Pacific Group)
44123 (the London Midland Society)
47324 (the London Midland Society)
76017 (the Standard 4 Locomotive Group)

Former Longmoor Military Railway 0-6-0ST No 196 *Errol Lonsdale* shunts a permanent way train at Ropley. *M. Ricks*

Didcot Railway Centre

Location: Adjacent to BR station, Didcot, Oxfordshire. Access via station subway
Operating society/organisation: Great Western Society Ltd, Didcot Railway Centre, Didcot, Oxon
Telephone: Didcot (0235) 817200
Car park: Didcot BR station
Access by public transport: Didcot BR station

Locomotives

Name	*No*	*Origin*	*Class*	*Type*	*Built*
Trojan	1340	GWR	Avonside (1380)	0-4-0ST	1897
—	1466	GWR	1400	0-4-2T	1936
—	3650	GWR	5700	0-6-0PT	1939
—	3738	GWR	5700	0-6-0PT	1937
—	3822	GWR	2884	2-8-0	1940

On site facilities: GWR locomotive depot, replica GWR station, museum and broad gauge and TPO demonstrations. Refreshments and souvenir sales, rides are available on the demonstration lines (limited facilities Mondays to Fridays)
Public opening: Saturdays, Sundays and Bank Holidays 3 March-28 October. Mondays to Fridays 24 April-26 October. Steaming days on first and last Sunday of each month, Bank Holidays and all August Sundays and Wednesdays, Gala steamings 31 March, 1 April, 23/24 June, 29/30 September. Open 11.00-17.00 (winter 16.00)
Feature article references: RW July 1982 p346

Name	*No*	*Origin*	*Class*	*Type*	*Built*
—	4144	GWR	5100	2-6-2T	1946
Maindy Hall	4942	GWR	'Hall'	4-6-0	1929
—	5322	GWR	4300	2-6-0	1917
—	5572	GWR	4575	2-6-2T	1927
Nunney Castle	5029	GWR	'Castle'	4-6-0	1934
Drysllwyn Castle/ Earl Bathurst	5051	GWR	'Castle'	4-6-0	1936
Hinderton Hall	5900	GWR	'Hall'	4-6-0	1931
—	6106	GWR	6100	2-6-2T	1931
—	6697	GWR	5600	0-6-2T	1928
Burton Agnes Hall	6998	GWR	'Hall'	4-6-0	1949
—	7202	GWR	7200	2-8-2T	1934
Cookham Manor	7808	GWR	'Manor'	4-6-0	1938
—	1363	GWR	1361	0-6-0ST	1910
—	D7018	BR	35	B-B	1962
Pontyberem	2	Burry Port & Gwendraeth Valley Rly		0-6-0ST	1900
Shannon	5	Wantage Tramway		0-4-0WT	1857

Industrial locomotives

Name	*No*	*Builder*	*Type*	*Built*
Bonnie Prince Charlie	—	RSH (7544)	0-4-0ST	1949
—	47	RSH (7800)	0-6-0ST	1954
—	—	Hunslet (5238)	0-6-0DH	1962

Stock
Over 40 ex-GWR coaches are preserved along with numerous ex-GWR freight wagons

Owners
5 (on loan from the National Railway Museum)
D7018 (Diesel & Electric Group)

A typical Great Western scene, recreated at the Didcot Railway Centre.
Great Western Society

Southall Railway Centre

Location: Merrick Road, Southall adjacent to BR station
Operating society/organisation: GWR Preservation Group, Southall Railway Centre, Merrick Road, Southall, Middlesex
Telephone: 01-574-1529 R. A. Gorringe (Evening and weekend only)
Car park: Merrick Road
On site facilities: Shop and light refreshments. Brake van rides on steaming dates
Public opening: Steam days. 22*, 23 April; 7, 27/28 May; 15* July; 25/26*/27 August; 29/30 September; 27/28 October. Schools week 2-6 July. Service operates within centre limits. Open for viewing remaining weekends between above dates *DMU service on Brentford branch
Facilities for disabled: No notice required
Special notes: Additional rolling stock expected during 1984

Stock
1 GWR brake van
1 LMS parcels van
1 BP oil tank wagon

Locomotives

Name	*No*	*Origin*	*Class*	*Type*	*Built*
—	2885	GWR	2884	2-8-0	1938
—	4110	GWR	5101	2-6-2T	1936
—	9682	GWR	5700	0-6-0PT	1949

Industrial Locomotives

Name	*No*	*Builder*	*Type*	*Built*
—	—	AEC Southall	4wDM	1938
Birkenhead	7386	RSH (7386)	0-4-0ST	1948
Francis Baily of Thatham	AD251	Ruston	0-4-0DM	1957
—	2	Peckett (2100)	0-4-0ST	1949

***Birkenhead* with No 9682 in the foreground.** *A. C. Butcher*

Romney, Hythe and Dymchurch Railway

Headquarters: Romney, Hythe and Dymchurch Railway, New Romney station, Kent
Telephone: New Romney 62353
Main station: Hythe
Other public stations: Dymchurch, Jefferstone Lane, New Romney, Romney Sands, Dungeness
Car parks: Hythe, Dymchurch, New Romney, Dymchurch, Dungeness
Access by public transport: Sandling Junction BR station (1½ miles), Folkestone Central BR station — 4 miles: bus connection from Folkestone bus station
Refreshment facilities: New Romney, Dungeness. Also in observation coach on certain trains
Souvenir shops: Hythe, Dymchurch, New Romney
Museum: New Romney
Depot: New Romney

Locomotives

Name	*No*	*Builder*	*Type*	*Built*
Green Goddess	1	Davey Paxman	4-6-2	1925
Northern Chief	2	Davey Paxman	4-6-2	1925
Southern Maid	3	Davey Paxman	4-6-2	1926
The Bug	4	Krauss	0-4-0T	1926
Hercules	5	Davey Paxman	4-8-2	1926
Samson	6	Davey Paxman	4-8-2	1926
Typhoon	7	Davey Paxman	4-6-2	1926
Hurricane	8	Davey Paxman	4-6-2	1926
Winston Churchill	9	YEC	4-6-2	1931
Doctor Syn	10	YEC	4-6-2	1931
Black Prince	11	Krupp	4-6-2	1937
—	12	TMA Birmingham	Bo-Bo	1983
—	PW1	M/Rail (7059)	4wDM	1938
—	PW2	RH&DR	4wPM	1965
Redgauntlet	PW3	RH&DR	4wPM	1975

Passenger trains: 15in gauge line. Train frequency depends on the time of year: maximum frequency is 45 minutes
Length of line: $13\frac{1}{2}$ miles
Period of public operation: Daily from Easter until end of September, and at weekends in March and October
Special notes: Children under 14 years will travel at $\frac{1}{3}$ fare. Cheap return fares are available on Friday mornings. Model railway and exhibition at New Romney. Parties can be catered for at New Romney

Stock
45 bogie coaches
14 open bogie coaches
3 semi-open coaches
40 assorted wagons

No 9 *Winston Churchill* accelerates away from Britannia points with the 17.10 Dungeness-Hythe. *P. H. Groom*

Sittingbourne and Kemsley Light Railway

Headquarters: Sittingbourne & Kemsley Light Railway Ltd, The Walk, Milton Regis, Sittingbourne, Kent
Telephone: Sittingbourne 24899 (operating times only)
Medway 32320 (other times)
Main station: Sittingbourne
Car park: Sittingbourne
Access by public transport: Sittingbourne BR station, A2 and M2 roads
Refreshment facilities: Kemsley Down
Souvenir shop: Sittingbourne
Depot: Kemsley Down (access by rail only)
Passenger trains: 2ft 6in gauge ex-industrial line Sittingbourne-Kemsley Down (2 miles)
Period of public operation: All bank holiday Saturdays and Sundays 21 July to 25 August, Sundays 15 April to 7 October, Good Friday, all bank holiday Mondays, Tuesdays, Wednesdays and Thursdays 31 July to 30 August. Father Christmas steam specials 16, 23, 30 and Boxing Day 26 December also Tuesday 1 January 1985
Special notes: There is no public access to Kemsley Down other than by the railway on operating dates. When the line is closed all stock is stored in security compounds, on the mill premises. Family ticket available, special rates for parties and senior citizens

Locomotives

Name	*No*	*Builder*	*Type*	*Built*
Alpha	—	Bagnall (2472)	0-6-2T	1932
Triumph	—	Bagnall (2511)	0-6-2T	1934
Superb	—	Bagnall (2624)	0-6-2T	1940
Unique	—	Bagnall (2216)	2-4-0F	1924
Premier	—	K/Stuart (886)	0-4-2ST	1905
Leader	—	K/Stuart (926)	0-4-2ST	1905
Melior	—	K/Stuart (4219)	0-4-2ST	1924
Edward Lloyd	—	R/Hornsby (435403)	4wDM	1961
Victor	—	Hunslet (614)	4wDM	1953

Industrial standard gauge locomotives

Name	*No*	*Builder*	*Type*	*Built*
—	4	H/Leslie (3718)	0-4-0ST	1928
Bear	—	Peckett (614)	0-4-0ST	1896
—	1	A/Barclay (1876)	0-4-0F	1925

Stock
10 bogie coaches (4 ex-Chattenden & Upnor Railway)
2 open coaches
Various wagons

Chalk Pits Museum

Narrow Gauge and Industrial Railway Collection (incorporating the Brockham Museum of Narrow Gauge Railways)

Location: Houghton Bridge, Amberley, West Sussex (3 miles north of Arundel). On B2139. Adjacent to Amberley BR(SR) station
Operating society/organisation: Southern Industrial History Centre Trust, Chalk Pits Museum, Houghton Bridge, Amberley, Arundel, West Sussex BN18 9LT
Telephone: Bury (079 881) 370 (Museum office)
Car park: Adjacent to Amberley Station
On site facilities: Shop, light refreshments, audio-visual show
Public opening: Wednesday to Sunday (inclusive) each week, and Bank Holiday Mondays, 11.00-17.00, 1 April-28 October 1984
Special Notes: The NG&IR Collection is part of an open air industrial museum set in 36 acres of the former Pepper & Co chalk pits. Displays include working potter and blacksmith, stationary engines, historic radio collection, and veteran Southdown buses. A 2ft 0in gauge quarry railway is demonstrated when possible. Late in 1981, the Museum was approached by the Trustees of the Brockham Museum with a view to transferring the entire collection to the Chalk Pits, and all exhibits have now been moved. At present, a second 2ft 0in gauge line is under construction using volunteers and a MSC Community Scheme and this will be used for carrying passengers in genuine workmen's vehicles hauled when possible by the restored steam locomotive *Polar Bear*. Passenger operation started on 17 April 1983, and the 500yd line, newly constructed on a winding 'shelf' formation in pleasant woodland, will be completed early in the 1984 season. For latest position and steam operating dates contact the museum office

Locomotives

Name	*No*	*Builder*	*Type*	*Built*
Polar Bear	—	Bagnall (1781)	2-4-0T	1905
Peter	—	Bagnall (2067)	0-4-0ST	1918
Townsend Hook	4	F/Jennings (172L)	0-4-0T	1880
William Finlay	5	F/Jennings (173L)	0-4-0T	1880
Scaldwell	—	Peckett (1316)	0-6-0ST	1913
—	23†	Spence	0-4-0T	1921
—	—	Decauville (1126)	0-4-0T	1950
Monty	(6)	Orenstein & Koppel (7269)	4wDM	1936
The Major	(7)	Orenstein & Koppel (7741)	4wDM	1937
—	2	Ransomes & Rapier (80)	4wDM	1937
—	—	Hudson-Hunslet (3097)	4wDM	1944
—	2	R/Hornsby (166024)	4wDM	1933
—	3041	M/Rail (Simplex) (1320)	4wDm (ex-PM)	1918
Peldon	—	John Fowler (21295)	4wDM	1936
Redland	—	Orenstein & Koppel (6193)	4wDM	1937
—	—	Lister (35421)	4wPM	1949
—	(LR 2593)	M/Rail (Simplex) (872)	4wPM	1918
—	—	M/Rail (Simplex) (10161)	4wDM	1949
—	—	M/Rail (Simplex) (11001)	4wDM	1951
CCSW	—	Hibberd (1980)	4wDM	1936
Thakeham Tiles	No 3	Hudson-Hunslet (2208)	4wDM	1941
Thakeham Tiles	No 4	Hudson-Hunslet (3653)	4wDM	1948
—	—	Hudswell Clarke (DM686)	0-4-0DM	1948
—	—	Hudson-Hunslet	4wDM	—
—	18	R/Hornsby (187081)	4wDM	1937
—	—	Hudson-Hunslet (2536)	4wDM	1941
—	—	Lister (33937)	4wDM	1949
—	—	Orenstein & Koppel (5926)	4wDM	1935
—	—	R/Hornsby (172892)	4wDM	1934
—	WD 904	Wickham (3403)	2w+2PMR	1943
—	2	Wingrove & Rogers (5031)	4wBE	1953
—	—	Wingrove & Rogers (5034)	4wBE	1953
—	—	Wingrove & Rogers (4998)	4wBE	1953
—	—	Wingrove & Rogers (T8033)	0-4-0BE	1979

†Includes hoist and 'haulage truck' for conversion to 5ft 3in gauge

Stock
2 Penrhyn Quarry Railway 4-wheel coaches (1ft 10$\frac{3}{4}$in gauge)
RAF Fauld bogie coach (1940) (2ft gauge)
Rye & Camber Tramway bogie coach (incomplete) (1895) (3ft gauge)
Groudle Glen Railway 4-wheel coach (1896) (2ft gauge)
60 other varied pieces of rolling stock of 12 different gauges ranging from 1ft 6in to 3ft 2$\frac{1}{4}$in plus numerous miscellaneous exhibits including track, signals etc

Hollycombe Woodland Railway

Location: Hollycombe House, near Liphook
Operating society/organisation: J. M. Baldock, Hollycombe House, Liphook, Hants GU30 7LP
Telephone: Liphook 723233
Car park: On site
Access by public transport: Liphook BR station
On site facilities: Museum, shop and refreshments
Public opening: Sundays and bank holidays Easter-end September, 14.00-18.00

A/Barclay (1995) 0-4-0T No 1 *Caledonia.* *D. Cox*

Science Museum

Location: South Kensington
Operating society/organisation: Science Museum, Exhibition Road, South Kensington, London SW7
Telephone: 01-589 3459
Access by public transport: South Kensington underground station
On site facilities: Small book shop and refreshments
Public opening: Weekdays 10.00-18.00, Sundays 14.30-18.00 (admission free)
Special notes: Static exhibits only

Stock
LPTB underground coach, No 3327 (built 1927)

Locomotives

Name	*No*	*Origin*	*Class*	*Type*	*Built*
Caerphilly Castle	4073	GWR	'Castle'	4-6-0	1923
Deltic	—	E/Electric	—	Co-Co	1955
Rocket	—	L&MR	—	0-2-2	1829
Sans Pareil	—	L&MR	—	0-4-0	1829
	1	C&SLR	—	4wE	1890
Puffing Billy	—	Wylam Colliery	—	4w	1813

Industrial locomotive

Name	*No*	*Builder*	*Type*	*Built*
Bauxite	2	B/Hawthorn (305)	0-4-0ST	1874

London Transport Museum

Location: Covent Garden, London WC2
Operating society/organisation: London Transport Executive
Telephone: 01-379 6344
Access by public transport: Underground to Covent Garden, Leicester Square or Charing Cross. Buses to Strand or Aldwych
On site facilities: Museum shop, lecture theatre and research library (by appointment)
Public opening: Daily 10.00-18.00 (last admissions 17.15). Closed Christmas Day, Boxing Day. Reduced admission prices for children, students, senior citizens and pre-booked parties
Special notes: The museum was opened in the converted Flower Market in March 1980. The displays cover nearly two centuries of public transport in London. Visitors can operate the controls of a tram, a bus, an Underground train, signals and points. In addition to the vehicles and rolling stock there are models, signs, posters, paintings, audio-visual displays and a 1906 Otis lift car. At certain times there will be films, lectures and temporary exhibitions. In addition to the vehicles on display there is a growing reserve collection

Locomotives

Name	*No*	*Origin*	*Class*	*Type*	*Built*
	23	Met Rly	A	4-4-0T	1866
John Hampden	5	Met Rly		Bo-Bo	1922

Industrial locomotive

Origin	*Builder*	*Type*	*Built*
Wotton Tramway	A/Porter (807)	0-4-0TG	1872

Electric stock
No 4248 District Rly Q23 stock driving motor coach 1923
No 11182 LPTB 1938 stock driving motor coach
No 400 Met Rly bogie stock coach 1899
No 30 City & South London Rly 'Padded Cell' coach 1890
Great Northern Piccadilly & Brompton Railway 'Gate stock' car 1906

Stock
1 Met Rly milk van
3 electric trams
3 horse buses
8 motor buses
2 trolleybuses

SOUTH-WEST

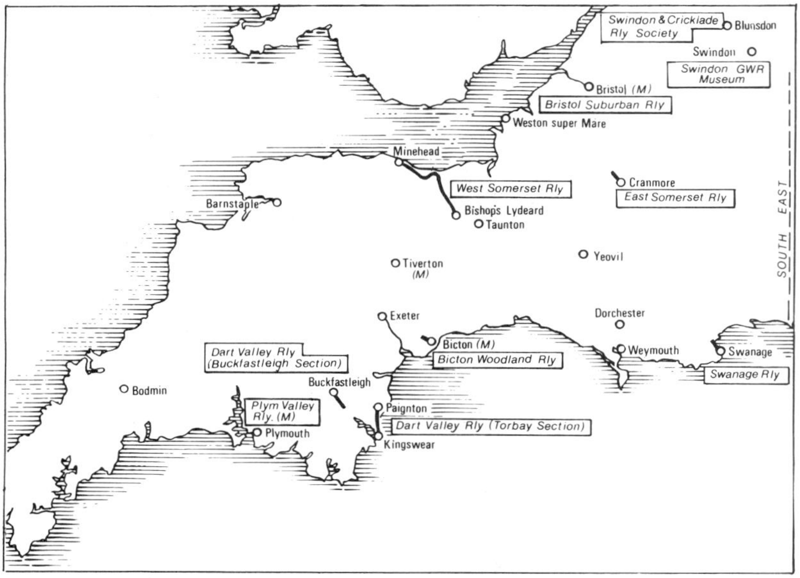

Dart Valley Railway (Torbay section)

Headquarters: Paignton Queen's Park station, Paignton, Devon
Telephone: Paignton 555872
Main station: Paignton Queen's Park
Other public stations: Goodrington, Churston, Kingswear (for Dartmouth)
Car parks: Paignton municipal car park, Dartmouth (ferry to Kingswear)
Access by public transport: Several local buses serve the station which is adjacent to the BR station at Paignton
Refreshment facilities: Kingswear
Museum: Buckfastleigh (Dart Valley line)
Depot: Buckfastleigh (Dart Valley line)
Passenger trains: Paignton-Kingswear (7 miles) views of Torbay and Dart estuary, 492 yd tunnel
Period of public operation: Telephone above for details

Locomotives

Name	*No*	*Origin*	*Class*	*Type*	*Built*
—	4588	GWR	4575	2-6-2T	1927
Goliath	5239	GWR	4200	2-8-0T	1924
Lydham Manor	7827	GWR	7800	4-6-0	1950
—	80064	BR	4MT	2-6-4T	1954
—	D2192	BR	03	0-6-0DM	1961
Western Fusilier	D1023	BR	52	C-C	1963

Industrial locomotive

Name	*No*	*Builder*	*Type*	*Built*
Enterprise	—	H/Clarke (D810)	0-6-0DM	1953

Stock

8 ex-BR Mk1 coaches
3 ER Suburban coaches (ex-Kings Cross)
1 Pullman observation coach
3 auto-coaches
Stock is sometimes transferred to and from the Dart Valley line

Note

D1023 (on loan from the National Railway Museum)

BR Standard 4MT 2-6-4T No 80064 leaves Paignton with the 14.35 for Kingswear, 2 April 1983. *C. F. Beatson*

GWR 0-6-0PT No 1638 hauls its three-coach train alongside the River Dart.
D. E. Canning

Dart Valley Railway (Buckfastleigh section)

Headquarters: Dart Valley Railway, Buckfastleigh station, Buckfastleigh, Devon
Telephone: Buckfastleigh 42338
Main station: Buckfastleigh
Other public stations: Staverton Bridge, Totnes
Car park: Buckfastleigh
Access by public transport: Bus, 129 Plymouth-Torquay via Totnes; 188 from Newton Abbot A38 road between Exeter and Plymouth
Refreshment facilities: Buckfastleigh
Souvenir shop: Buckfastleigh
Museum: Buckfastleigh
Depot: Buckfastleigh
Passenger trains: Buckfastleigh-Totnes (7 miles) alongside the River Dart
Period of public operation: Telephone above for details
Feature article reference: TI No 40 p28

Locomotives

Name	*No*	*Origin*	*Class*	*Type*	*Built*
Bulliver	1420	GWR	1400	0-4-2T	1933
Ashburton	1450	GWR	1400	0-4-2T	1935
—	1369	GWR	1366	0-6-0PT	1934
Dartington	1638	GWR	1600	0-6-0PT	1951
—	4555	GWR	4500	2-6-2T	1924
Dumbleton Hall	4920	GWR	'Hall'	4-6-0	1929
—	6430	GWR	6400	0-6-0PT	1937
—	6435	GWR	6400	0-6-0PT	1937
—	30587	LSWR	0298	2-4-0WT	1874
Tiny	—	SDR	—	0-4-0VBT	1868

Industrial locomotives

Name	*No*	*Builder*	*Type*	*Built*
Ashley	1	Peckett (2031)	0-4-0ST	1942
Lady Angela	1690	Peckett (1690)	0-4-0ST	1926
—	—	Bagnall (2766)	0-6-0ST	1944
Maureen	—	Hunslet (2890)	0-6-0ST	1943
Glendower	—	Hunslet (3810)	0-6-0ST	1954
—	—	Fowler (421014)	0-4-0DM	1958

Note
30587 (on loan from the National Railway Museum)

Tiny, 7ft $0\frac{1}{4}$in gauge, part of the National Collection

Stock
4 ex-BR Mk1 coaches
12 ex-GWR coaches
1 steam crane

East Somerset Railway

Headquarters: East Somerset Railway, (Cranmore Railway Station) Shepton Mallet
Telephone: Cranmore 417
Main station: Cranmore
Car park: Cranmore
Refreshment facilities: Cranmore, Cranmore depot
Souvenir shop: Cranmore
On site facilities: Museum and signalbox art gallery
Depot: Cranmore West

Aerial view of No 92203 climbing towards Merryfield Lane from Cranmore.
Tuder Heawood/East Somerset Railway

Passenger trains: Cranmore West to Merryfield Lane and return ($1\frac{1}{2}$ miles)
Period of public operation: Depot open daily April to October, with trains running each Sunday, Public Holidays, Wednesdays in peak season and on certain Saturdays. Depot open weekends only November to March, with trains running on Sundays and other days during December
Facilities for disabled: Advance notice required
Special Notes: Trains are at present unable to run into Cranmore station. A footpath connects Cranmore station with the depot, which is adjacent to Cranmore West station

Stock
5 ex-BR Mk1 coaches
1 ex-LMS coach
1 ex-LNER (design) sleeping car
25 assorted wagons, mostly LMS and SR

Locomotives

Name	*No*	*Origin*	*Class*	*Type*	*Built*
Bluebell	323	SECR	P	0-6-0T	1910
—	6634	GWR	5600	0-6-2T	1928
—	32110	LBSCR	E1	0-6-0T	1877
—	47493	LMS	3F	0-6-0T	1927
The Green Knight	75029	BR	4MT	4-6-0	1954
Black Prince	92203	BR	9F	2-10-0	1959

Industrial locomotives

Name	*No*	*Builder*	*Type*	*Built*
Lord Fisher	1398	Barclay (1398)	0-4-0ST	1915
Glenfield	1719	Barclay (1719)	0-4-0ST	1920
—	4101	Dubs (4101)	0-4-0CT	1901
—	68005	RSH (7169)	0-6-0ST	1944

Owner
323 (Bluebell Railway Preservation Society)
6634 (the 6634 Locomotive Co)

West Somerset Railway

Headquarters: West Somerset Railway, The Railway Station, Minehead, Somerset
Telephone: Minehead 4996
Main station: Minehead
Other public stations: Dunster, Blue Anchor, Washford, Watchet, Williton, Stogumber, Crowcombe, Bishop's Lydeard
Car parks: Minehead, Williton, Bishops Lydeard. Some parking at all stations
Access by public transport: Nearest BR station, Taunton
Refreshment facilities: Minehead, Bishop's Lydeard (limited opening), Williton (limited opening), Watchet (limited opening)
Souvenir shops: Minehead, Bishop's Lydeard (limited opening)
Museum: Somerset & Dorset Railway Museum Trust, Washford
Depots: Bishop's Lydeard, Williton, Washford, Minehead
Passenger trains: Stopping trains to Williton (10 miles) or Bishops Lydeard (20 miles).
Period of public operation: Daily May-September, limited service in other months. Some trains to/from Bishops Lydeard have connecting bus link with Taunton and BR

Locomotives

Name	*No*	*Origin*	*Class*	*Type*	*Built*
—	88	S&DJR	7F	2-8-0	1925
—	4561	GWR	4500	2-6-2T	1924
—	5542	GWR	4575	2-6-2T	1928
—	6412	GWR	6400	0-6-0PT	1934
—	D7017	BR	35	B-B	1962
—	D2271	BR	04	0-6-0DM	1952
—	D2994	BR	07	0-6-0DE	1962
—	D9526	BR	14	0-6-0DH	1964
—	D9551	BR	14	0-6-0DH	1965

Industrial locomotives

Name	*No*	*Builder*	*Type*	*Built*
Portbury	S3	Avonside (1764)	0-6-0ST	1917
Vulcan	2994	Bagnall (2994)	0-6-0ST	1950
Victor	2996	Bagnall (2996)	0-6-0ST	1951
—	—	Bagnall (2473)	0-4-0ST	1932
Jennifer	20	H/Clarke (1731)	0-6-0T	1942
Isabel	—	H/Leslie (3437)	0-6-0ST	1919
Kilmersdon	—	Peckett (1788)	0-4-0ST	1929
—	24	Ruston (210479)	4wDM	1941
—	—	Ruston (183062)	4wDM	1937

'Hymek' No D7017 and No 2994 *Vulcan* double-head the 'West Somerset Wanderer', the longest train to date on the WSR. *S. J. Edge*

Facilities for disabled: Parking space level with entrance. No steps to shop or booking office, level access to toilets (no special facilities however). Catering facilities can be reached without difficulties. Groups can be catered for. Advanced booking advised to guarantee facilities. No special facilities on train but assistance available

Owners
S3 (the Somerset & Dorset Museum Trust)
Isabel (the Somerset & Dorset Museum Trust)
Kilmersdon (the Somerset & Dorset Museum Trust)
88 (the Somerset & Dorset Museum Trust)
Bagnall 2473 (the Somerset & Dorset Museum Trust)
D7017 and D9526 (the Diesel and Electric Group)
5542 (the 5542 Fund)

Stock
13 ex-BR Mk1 coaches
2 ex-BR Restaurant cars
1 ex-BR suburban coach
7 ex-GWR camping coaches
1 ex-LNER coach
1 ex-SR 'Ironclad' coach
2 Park Royal 2-car diesel units
1 Craven 2-car diesel unit
1 ex-GWR Hawksworth coach
1 ex-LMS parcels van
More than 40 freight vehicles

Swanage Railway Centre

Location: Swanage station
Operating society/organisation: Swanage Railway Co Ltd, Station Master's House, Railway Station, Swanage, Dorset
Car park: Swanage
Access by public transport: Hants & Dorset buses from Bournemouth, Poole and Wareham stop outside station
On site facilities: Shop and light refreshments. Shop open daily mid-May-mid-September
Public opening: Open for viewing Saturday and Sundays and bank holidays (except Christmas). Trains run; Saturdays July, August and September; Sundays April-September. Daily throughout August
Length of line: 1 mile
Facilities for disabled: Access to station, shop and toilets
Feature article reference: TI No 41 p22

Stock
1 Bulleid coach
LSWR coach body
3 ex-SR vans
2 ex-SR coaches
3 ex-BR Mk1 coaches
LNWR CCT
GWR hand crane
1 ex-Brighton Belle Pullman No 288
2 ex-SR Maunsell coaches
1 ex-LMS coach
20 various types of wagons

Locomotives

Name	*No*	*Origin*	*Class*	*Type*	*Built*
—	6695	GWR	5600	0-6-2T	1928
*Holland America Line**	35022	SR	MN	4-6-2	1948
—	80078	BR	4MT	2-6-4T	1954
—	80104*	BR	4MT	2-6-4T	1955

Industrial locomotives

Name	*No*	*Builder*	*Type*	*Built*
—	—	Planet (2054)	4wPM	1938
Cunarder	1690	Hunslet (1690)	0-6-0ST	1931
—	—	Peckett (2150)	0-6-0ST	1954
May	2	Fowler (4210132)	0-4-0DM	1957
Beryl	—	Planet	4wD	1937
—	319290	R/Hornsby (319290)	4wDM	1953

*Not on site

Owners
6695 (the Great Western Railway Preservation Group)
80078 and 80104 (the Southern Steam Trust)
Cunarder (owned by 1708 Locomotive Preservation Trust Ltd)
35022 (the Merchant Navy Locomotive Group)

Hunslet 0-6-0ST *Cunarder* hauls its two-coach train into Swanage on 11 September 1983. *M. H. C. Baker*

Bristol Suburban Railway

Headquarters: Bitton Railway Co Ltd, Bitton Station, Bristol, Avon
Main station: Bitton
Car park: Bitton
Access by public transport: Bristol Omnibus service No 332 Bath-Bristol. No 58 Ashton Drive-Park Estate
On site facilities: Toilets, snack bar
Public opening: Every weekend. In steam first Sunday in month, Easter-October. Plus Bank Holidays. Every weekend in December

Stock
4 ex-BR Mk1 coach
1 ex-BR Mk1 Restaurant Coach
1 ex-GWR coach
2 ex-GER coach chassis
3 open wagons
3 box vans
3 refrigerated box vans
1 ex-GWR Fruit 'C'
1 ex-GWR ballast wagon
1 ex-GWR hand crane and match truck

Locomotive

Name	*No*	*Origin*	*Class*	*Type*	*Built*
—	45379	LMS	5MT	4-6-0	1937

Industrial locomotives

Name	*No*	*Builder*	*Type*	*Built*
Edwin Hulse	2	Avonside (1798)	0-6-0ST	1918
—	3	F/Walker (242)	0-6-0ST	1874
Littleton No 5	—	M/Wardle (2018)	0-6-0ST	1922
Fonmon	—	Peckett (1936)	0-6-0ST	1924
—	—	RSH (7151)	0-6-0T	1944
—	—	R/Hornsby (235519)	4wDM	1945
—	—	Baguley/Drewry (2153)	0-4-0	1941

Manning Wardle 0-6-0ST *Littleton No 5*.
G. Scott-Lowe

Bristol Industrial Museum

Location: Princes Wharf, Bristol
Operating society/organisation: Bristol Industrial Museum, Princes Wharf, Bristol, Avon BS1 4RN
Telephone: Bristol 299771
Car parks: Available nearby
Access by public transport: Buses to centre of town
On site facilities: Shop
Public opening: Saturday-Wednesday 10.00-13.00; 14.00-17.00
Special notes: Operation of railway on advertised weekends only

Plym Valley Railway

Location: 5 miles from centre of Plymouth, Devon, north of A38
Operating society/organisation: Plym Valley Railway, Coy Pool, Plymouth, Devon
Telephone: Plymouth 337752

The Plym Valley is a comparatively new preservation society and is having to start from scratch. This will be the site of the main depot, April 1983.

Access by public transport: Buses from Plymouth, Nos 20, 21, 22, 23, 58, 59
On site facilities: Shop and refreshments at Marsh Mills, Coy Pool
Public opening: Site open most days from 10.00
Special notes: Visitors are advised that, at the moment, the railway and its locomotives are still under restoration. Prospective visitors are advised to take the advice of their guides.
Feature article references: TI No 42 p4

Locomotives

Name	No	Origin	Class	Type	Built
—	4160	GWR	41xx	2-6-2T	1948
Wadebridge	34007	SR	WC	4-6-2	1945
—	75079	BR	4MT	4-6-0	1956
—	D3002	BR	08	0-6-0DE	1953
*Western Lady**	D1048	BR	52	Co-Co	1962
—	4112†	SAR	GMAM	—	—

*Not on site, arrival date to be arranged, currently on display at Steamport, Southport
†Not on site, arrival date unknown

Swindon & Cricklade Railway

Location: Tadpole Lane, Blunsdon (approximately mid way between Blundson St Andrew and Purton)
Operating society/organisation: Swindon & Cricklade Railway, Mrs A. R. Palk, 5 Bradene Close, Wootton Bassett, Swindon, Wilts SN4 8DG
Telephone: Mrs A. R. Palk (Swindon 853166) or Blunsdon Station (Swindon 771615)
Station: Blunsdon
Car park: Tadpole Lane, Blunsdon
Refreshment facilities: Blunsdon station amenities building
Souvenir shop: Blunsdon station amenities building
Depot: Blunsdon
Public opening: Saturdays and Sundays throughout the year. Open Days during summer season commencing Easter
Passenger trains: Passenger services available on specified weekends throughout the summer season
Facilities for disabled: Access to shop and refreshments, adapted BR coach
Feature article reference: TI No 41 p8

Locomotive

Name	No	Origin	Class	Type	Built
Foremarke Hall	7903	GWR	'Hall'	4-6-0	1949
—	5637	GWR	56xx	0-6-2T	1924
Port Line	35027	SR	MN	4-6-2	1948

Industrial locomotives

Name	No	Builder	Type	Built
Gnundraclese	—	Fowler	0-4-0DM	—
—	—	Fowler (4210082)	0-4-0DM	1953
—	—	Fowler (4210105)	0-4-0DM	—
—	—	Fowler (21442)	0-4-0DM	1936
Richard Trevithic	—	A/Barclay (2354)	0-4-0ST	1955
—	—	K/Stuart (3063)	0-4-0WT	1917

Stock
4 BR coaches
1 GWR coach
Small selection of wagons
20 ton steam crane

Owners
7903 (the Foremarke Hall Locomotive Group)
35027 Port Line Locomotive Project

Former Great Western Railway coach now preserved at Blunsdon. *R. Palk*

Bicton Woodland Railway

Location: Bicton Gardens, near Sidmouth
Operating society/organisation: Bicton Woodland Railway, Bicton Gardens, East Budleigh, Budleigh Salterton, Devon
Telephone: Colaton Raleigh 68465
Car park: On site
Access by public transport: Buses pass half-hourly from Exeter, Exmouth, Sidmouth
On site facilities: Refreshments, shop, two museums, toilets, 18in gauge railway
Public opening: From 1 April
Facilities for disabled: Wheelchairs available. Special carriage for wheelchairs

Seaton & Colyford Electric Tramway

Location: Seaton, Devon
Operating society/organisation: Seaton & District Electric Tramway, Riverside Depot, Harbour Road, Seaton, Devon EX12 2NQ
Telephone: Seaton 21702
Access by public transport: Located near to centre of Seaton
On site facilities: Shop
Period of public operation: Daily

Swindon GWR Museum

Location: Faringdon Road, Swindon, Wiltshire
Operating society/organisation: Borough of Thamesdown, GWR Museum, Faringdon Road, Swindon, Wiltshire
Telephone: Swindon 26161 ext 3131
Car park: Swindon BR station and street parking
Access by public transport: Swindon BR (10minutes)
On site facilities: A selection of souvenirs is available
Public opening: Weekdays 10.00-17.00, Sundays 14.00-17.00. Closed Good Friday, Christmas Day, Boxing Day and New Year's Day
Special Notes: The Museum also houses a considerable number of photographs depicting scenes of the GWR.
Feature article reference: TI No 42 p10

Locomotives

Name	*No*	*Origin*	*Class*	*Type*	*Built*
—	2516	GWR	2301	0-6-0	1887
City of Truro	3717	GWR	'City'	4-4-0	1903
Lode Star	4003	GWR	'Star'	4-6-0	1907
—	9400	GWR	9400	0-6-0PT	1947
*North Star**	—	GWR	—	2-2-2	1837

*Broad gauge replica

Owners
All locomotives are part of the National Railway Museum Collection

Tiverton Museum

Location: Tiverton, Devon
Operating society/organisation: Tiverton Museum Society, St Andrew Street, Tiverton, Devon EX16 6PH
Telephone: Tiverton 256295 or (Curator) 820517
Car park: Adjoining
Access by public transport: Bus from Exeter
On site facilities: Museum, shop and toilets
Public opening: All year except Sundays, bank holidays and Christmas break, 10.30-4.30
Special notes: Facilities for disabled

WALES

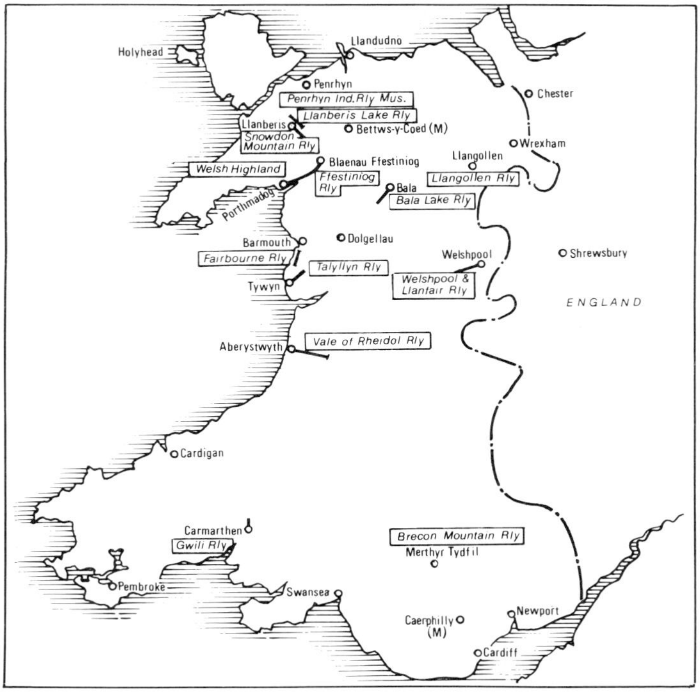

Gwili Railway/Rheilffordd Gwili

Headquarters: Gwili Railway Company Limited, Bronwydd Arms station, Bronwydd Arms, Carmarthen, Dyfed
Telephone: Swansea (0792) 201107
Main station: Bronwydd Arms
Other public stations: Cwmdwyfran, Penybont. To be opened: Llwyfan Cerrig
Car park: Bronwydd Arms
Access by public transport: Carmarthen BR station, then Crossville bus service No S44. A484 road. (Not Sundays)
Refreshment facilities: Bronwydd Arms, Llwyfan Cerrig (picnic site). Bar on train
Souvenir shop: Bronwydd Arms
Depot: Some stock at 'Ironrails', Carmarthen
Passenger trains: 3-mile return journey Bronwydd Arms-Penybont, regular hourly or 45-minute service
Period of public operation: Easter 21-24 April; May Day 7 May; Spring Bank Holiday 26-29 May; Sundays 3 June-30 September; Saturdays 7 July-1 September; Monday, Tuesday and Wednesdays in August.
Special notes: School specials in June and July. Santa specials in December

Locomotives

Name	*No*	*Origin*	*Class*	*Type*	*Built*
Dinmore Manor	7820	GWR	'Manor'	4-6-0	1950

Industrial locomotives

Name	*No*	*Builder*	*Type*	*Built*
—	1	H/Clark (1885)	0-6-0ST	1955
Merlin/Myrddin	—	Peckett (1967)	0-4-0ST	1939
—	1903	Peckett (1903)	0-4-0ST	1936
—	—	R/Hornsby (207103)	4wDM	1941
Olwen	7058	RSH (7058)	0-4-0ST	1942
—	71516	RSH (7170)	0-6-0ST	1944
—	—	YE(2779)	0-4-0DE	1960

Stock

1 ex-BR diesel unit trailer car
1 ex-BR Mk1 coach
2 ex-BR suburban coaches
1 ex-BR griddle car
1 ex-TVR coach
Diesel rail crane
Various vans and open wagons

Llangollen Railway Society

Location: Llangollen station, A542 from Ruabon, A5 from Shrewsbury, A5 from Betws y Coed
Operating society/organisation: Llangollen Railway Society Ltd, Llangollen station, Llangollen, Clwyd
Telephone: Llangollen 860951
Main station: Llangollen
Car park: Llangollen (Market Street)
Access by public transport: Nearest station: Ruabon (2hr service), then Crosville bus service No D1 to Llangollen or Nos D93/D94
Refreshment facilities: Llangollen
Souvenir shop: Llangollen
Passenger trains: Length of track 1-mile
Period of public operation: Sundays Easter-30 September, 13.00-17.30, 45 minute intervals also operates bank holidays and during International Eisteddfod week in July. Open for viewing weekends throughout the year plus daily during the tourist season
Facilities for disabled: In shop and refreshment room. Special coach for disabled persons. No special facilities for toilet access

Stock
3 coaches
4 wagons
1 GWR steam crane (working)
1 GWR siphon G
2 GWR brake vans
1 SR 'BY' parcels van
2 tank wagons
1 LNER parcels van
1 BR Fruit van

Locomotives

Name	*No*	*Origin*	*Class*	Type	*Built*
—	7754	GWR	5700	0-6-0PT	1930
—	7298	LMS	3F	0-6-0T	1924

Industrial locomotives

Name	*No*	*Builder*	*Type*	*Built*
Eliseg	—	Fowler (22753)	0-4-0DM	1939
—	—	Fowler (400007)	0-4-0DM	1947
Richboro	—	H/Clarke (1243)	0-6-0T	1917
—	1243	Hunslet (1243)	0-6-0T	1917
Austin No1	—	Kitson (5439)	0-6-0ST	1932
—	14	H/Clarke (D1012)	0-4-0DM	1956
—	—	North British (27734)	0-4-0DH	1958
—	—	Peckett (1567)	0-6-0ST	1920

***Austin No 1* approaching Llangollen.**
B. Morrison

Caerphilly Railway Society

Location: Harold Wilson Industrial Estate
Operating society/organisation: Caerphilly Railway Society Ltd, Harold Wilson Industrial Estate, Van Road, Caerphilly, Mid-Glamorgan
Car park: At the site
Access by public transport: The depot is 1 mile from Caerphilly rail and bus stations
On site facilities: Souvenir shop and light refreshments available on steam days only
Public opening: Static displays on Sundays 14.00-17.00, also steam days as advertised

Taff Vale Railway No 28 as restored by the Caerphilly Railway Society, May 1983.
M. Brown

The railway that sparked off the preservation of Britain's heritage was the Talyllyn Railway in Wales. Following the takeover by preservationists in 1951 it is now one of the most popular tourist attractions in the principality. Former Corris Railway 0-4-2ST *Sir Haydn* leaves Tywyn Pendre on 31 August 1981. *Hugh Ballantyne*

Stock
3 freight wagons
1 ex-BR Mk1 coach
1 staff and tool van
1 ex-GWR rail mounted crane
1 ex-GWR brake van
2 oil tank wagons

Locomotives

Name	*No*	*Origin*	*Class*	*Type*	*Built*
—	41312	BR	2MT	2-6-2T	1952
—	28	TVR	01	0-6-2T	1897

Industrial locomotives

Name	*No*	*Builder*	*Type*	*Built*
Victory	—	Barclay (2201)	0-4-0ST	1945
Forester	—	Barclay (1260)	0-4-0ST	1911
Desmond	—	Avonside (1498)	0-4-0ST	1906
—	—	RSH (7705)	0-4-0ST	1952
Haulwen	—	V/Foundry (5272)	0-6-0ST	1945
Deighton	—	YEC (2731)	0-4-0DE	1959

Owner
28 (the National Railway Museum, on loan from the Museum of Wales)

Bala Lake Railway (Rheilffordd Llyn Tegid)

Headquarters: Rheilffordd Llyn Tegid (Bala Lake Railway) Llanuwchllyn, Bala, Gwynedd
Telephone: Llanuwchllyn 666
Main station: Llanuwchllyn
Other public stations: Llangower, Bala
Car parks: Llanuwchllyn, Llangower and Bala town centre
Access by public transport: Crosville bus services Nos D93 and D94 to both Bala and Llanuwchllyn (from Wrexham or Barmouth)
Refreshment facilities: Llanuwchllyn. Large picnic site with toilet facilities by lake at Llangower
Souvenir shop: Llanuwchllyn
Museum: Large collection of antique railway equipment
Depot: Llanuwchllyn
Passenger trains: 1ft 11⅝in gauge line Llanuwchllyn — Bala (4½ miles). Journey takes 25 minutes in each direction
Period of public operation: Daily Easter until end of September then weekends until mid-October
Special notes: Two train operation over Bank Holidays and daily during August. Special parties may just turn up, but a day's notice for large parties would be helpful

Industrial Locomotives

Name	*No*	*Builder*	*Type*	*Built*
Jonathan	—	Hunslet (678)	0-4-0ST	1898
Holy War	—	Hunslet (779)	0-4-0ST	1902
Maid Marian	—	Hunslet (822)	0-4-0ST	1903
Meirionnydd	—	Severn Lamb (7322)	Bo-Bo	1973
Alice	—	Hunslet (780)	0-4-0ST	1902
Dryw Bach	—	K/Stuart (3114)	0-4-0ST	1918
Chilmark	—	R/Hornsby (194771)	4wDM	1939
—	—	R/Hornsby (200744)	4wDM	1940
—	—	Lister (44052)	4wDM	1958
—	—	Hudson (38384)	4wDM	1930
—	—	Motorail (5821)	4wDM	1934
—	—	R/Hornsby (209430)	4wDM	1942
—	—	R/Hornsby (189972)	4wDM	1938
—	—	Hibberd (FH2544)	4wDM	1941
—	—	Hunslet (758248)	4wDM	1940
—	—	R/Hornsby (200948)	4wDM	1940
—	—	R/Hornsby (283512)	4wDM	1949

Maid Marian **outside the signalbox at Llanuwchllyn.** *P. Ward*

Brecon Mountain Railway

Headquarters: Brecon Mountain Railway, Pontsticill station, Merthyr Tydfil, Mid Glamorgan
Telephone: Merthyr Tydfil (0685) 4854
Main station: Pant
Car park: Pant station
Access by public transport: Merthyr Tydfil Borough Council omnibus to Pant Cemetery — ½ hourly frequency from Merthyr bus station. BR rail service to Merthyr from Cardiff Central
Refreshment facilities: Not yet finalised but refreshments will be available
Facilities for disabled: Toilets
Depot: Pontsticill
Length of line: 2 miles
Special notes: 1ft 11¾in gauge

Stock
9 bogie wagons
2 balcony end 39 seat coaches
2 balcony end 40 seat coaches
Miscellaneous rail carrying and ballast wagons
South African Railways Box Car

Locomotives

Name	*No*	*Builder*	*Type*	*Built*
—	—	Baldwin (61269)	4-6-2	1930
Sybil	—	Hunslet (827)	0-4-0ST	1903
Graf Schwerin-Lowitz	99.3353	Arn Jung (1261)	0-6-2WT	1908
—	—	O&K (12722)	0-4-0WT	1936
Redstone	—	Redstone	0-4-0VBT	1905
—	—	R/Hornsby (425798)	4wDM	1958
—	—	R/Hornsby (444207)	4wDM	1961
Pendyffryn	—	de Winton	0-4-0VBT	1894
Rhydychen	—	Simplex (11177)	4wDM	1961
Garret	—	M/Rail (7902)	4wDM	1939

***Graf Schwerin-Lowitz* with a Pant-Pontsticill train.** *M. Floate*

Fairbourne Railway

Headquarters: Fairbourne Railway Ltd, Beach Road, Fairbourne, Gwynedd, LL38 2EX
Telephone: 0341-250362
Main station: Fairbourne
Other public stations: Barmouth Ferry, Public halts at Bathing Beach, Golf House, Passing Loop and Penrhyn Bridge
Car parks: Fairbourne and adjacent to Bathing Beach & Golf House halts
Access by public transport: Fairbourne BR station. Crossville bus service No S28 Dolgellau-Towyn A493 road
Refreshment facilities: Fairbourne and Ferry — with picnic site
Souvenir shop: Fairbourne
Depot: Fairbourne
Passenger trains: 15in gauge line Fairbourne-Barmouth Ferry (just under 2 miles). Journey time approx 20 minutes each way. Trains connect with Barmouth Ferry
Period of public operation: Easter to end of October

Locomotives

Name	*No*	*Builder*	*Type*	*Built*
Count Louis	—	B/Lowke (32)	4-4-2	1924
Ernest W. Twining	—	G&S (10)	4-6-2	1949
Katie	—	G&S (14)	2-4-2	1954
Sian	—	Guest (18)	2-4-2	1963
Rachel	—	G&S (15)	0-6-0DM	1959
Sylvia	—	G&S (14A)	Bo-BoPH	1961
Gwril	—	Lister (20886)	4wPM	1941

Stock
17 coaches
1 canteen coach
8 wagons (including 2 bogie tipper wagons)

Special notes: A flag is flown at Barmouth Ferry when trains are running. During inclement weather the service may be restricted or cancelled. Extra trains and special parties by arrangement with the manager

Ian Allan sponsor the annual 'Best Restored Station Competition', the winner in 1980 was the Dart Valley Railway's Staverton Bridge station. *Myles Cooper*

The Middleton Railway in Leeds was the first standard gauge line to be preserved, but the honour of the first to carry passengers goes to the Bluebell Railway in Sussex. No 30583 seen here in BR livery dates from 1882. *Brian Stephenson*

Ffestiniog Railway

Headquarters: Ffestiniog Railway, Harbour station, Porthmadog, Gwynedd, LL49 9NF
Telephone: Porthmadog 2384/2340
Main station: Porthmadog Harbour, Blaenau Ffestiniog
Other public stations: Minffordd, Penrhyn, Tan-y-Bwlch, Tanygrisiau
Car parks: Porthmadog, Tan-y-Bwlch, Tanygrisiau, Blaenau Ffestiniog
Access by public transport: Minffordd and Blaenau Ffestiniog BR stations. Porthmadog, Minffordd and Tanygrisiau and Blaenau Ffestiniog served by local buses
Refreshment facilities: Restuaurant at Porthmadog, buffets at Tan-y-Bwlch (summer only) and Blaenau Ffestiniog, also on most trains
Souvenir shops: Porthmadog, Tan-y-Bwlch, Blaenau Ffestiniog
Museum: Porthmadog
Depot: Boston Lodge
Passenger trains: 1ft 11½in gauge line Porthmadog-Blaenau Ffestiniog
Length of line: 13½ miles
Period of public operation: Weekends February-March. Daily April-October, and Christmas
Facilities for disabled: Porthmadog and Blaenau Ffestiniog easily accessible for wheelchairs. Facilities on trains for disabled in wheelchairs by prior arrangement
Special notes: Reduced rates available for early or late return trains
Feature article references: RW July 1982 p366; RW October 1983 p534; TI No 46 p10; TI No 47 p16

Locomotives

Name	*No*	*Builder*	*Type*	*Built*
Princess	1	G/England (199/200)	0-4-0STT	1863
Prince	2	G/England (?)	0-4-0STT	1863
Welsh Pony	—	G/England (234)	0-4-0STT	1867
Earl of Merioneth	—	FR (3)	0-4-4-0T	1979
Merddin Emrys	10	FR (1)	0-4-4-0T	1879
Moelwyn	—	Baldwin (49604)	2-4-0DM	1918
Blanche	—	Hunslet (589)	2-4-0STT	1893
Linda	—	Hunslet (590)	2-4-0STT	1893
Britomart	—	Hunslet (707)	0-4-0ST	1899
Mountaineer	—	Alco (57156)	2-6-2T	1917
Livingston Thompson†	3	FR(2)	0-4-4-0T	1886
—	—	Peckett (2050)	0-6-0ST	1944
—*	—	B/Peacock (5792)	0-4-0+0-4-0	1909
Upnor Castle	—	Hibberd (3687)	0-4-0DM	1954
Moel Hebog	—	Hunslet (4113)	0-4-0DM	1955
Mary Ann	—	M/Rail (596?)	0-4-0DM	1917

7 other 4wDM units
*on loan to National Railway Museum
†boiler unit only

Stock
27 bogie coaches
4 4-wheel coaches
2 brake vans, plus numerous service vehicles.

***Blanche* with the 14.05 Porthmadog-Blaneau Ffestiniog train at Gelliwiog, May 1982.** *J. Scrace*

Llanberis Lake Railway (Rheilfford Llyn Padarn)

Headquarters: Llanberis Lake Railway, Gilfach Ddu, Llanberis, Gwynedd LL55 4TY
Telephone: Llanberis (0286) 870549
Main station: Llanberis (Padarn Station/ Gilfachddu)
Other public stations: Cei Llydan
Car park: Llanberis (Padarn Station)
Refreshment facilities: Padarn Station
Souvenir shop: Padarn Station
Passenger trains: 1ft 11½in gauge line Llanberis-Penllyn-Llanberis
Length of line: 4 miles

***Elidir* runs round its train at Llanberis, 26 September 1983.** *C. C. Hall*

Facilities for disabled: Level approaches throughout shop, cafe and to train. Special toilet facilities provided. All disabled visitors welcomed
Period of public operation: Sundays to Friday Easter-October; plus Saturdays in July and August

Stock
13 bogie coaches
20 wagons

Industrial locomotives

Name	*No*	*Builder*	*Type*	*Built*
Elidir	1	Hunslet (493)	0-4-0ST	1889
Wild Aster	2	Hunslet (849)	0-4-0ST	1904
Dolbadarn	3	Hunslet (1430)	0-4-0ST	1922
Helen Kathryn	5	Henschel (28035)	0-4-0T	1948
Twll Coed	8	R/Hornsby (268878)	4wDM	1952
Dolgarrog	9	M/Rail (22154)	4wDM	1962
—	10	R/Hornsby (441427)	4wDM	1961
—	11	R/Hornsby (425 796)	4wDM	
AMW No 196	14	R/Hornsby (198 286)	4wDM	
AMW No 231	16	R/Hornsby (203031)	4wDM	
Garret	17	M/Rail (7902)	4wDM	1939
Braich	18	M/Rail (7927)	4wDM	1941
Llanelli	19	R/Hornsby (451901)	4wDM	1961

Snowdon Mountain Railway

Headquarters: Snowdon Mountain Railway, Llanberis, Gwynedd LL55-4TY
Telephone: Llanberis 870223
Main station: Llanberis
Other public stations: Summit
Car park: Llanberis
Access by public transport: Bangor BR station then by Crosville bus L1 or M5 to Caernarvon and there change to Crosville N99 to Llanberis
Refreshment facilities: Llanberis, Summit
Souvenir shops: Llanberis, Summit
Depot: Llanberis
Passenger trains: 80cm gauge line Llanberis-Summit. Journey time 60 minutes. Departures from Llanberis at 30 minute intervals during peak periods
Period of public operation: Daily Easter until early October. No weekend working early and late season
Length of line: $4\frac{3}{4}$ miles
Special notes: The only British rack and pinion railway. All trains are subject to weather and traffic restrictions. Special parties welcome by prior arrangement

Locomotives

Name	*No*	*Builder*	*Type*	*Built*
Enid	2	SLM (924)	0-4-2T	1895
Wyddfa	3	SLM (925)	0-4-2T	1895
Snowdon	4	SLM (988)	0-4-2T	1896
Moel Siabod	5	SLM (989)	0-4-2T	1896
Padarn	6	SLM (2838)	0-4-2T	1922
Ralph Sadler	7	SLM (2869)	0-4-2T	1923
Eryri	8	SLM (2870)	0-4-2T	1923

All the above were built by Swiss Locomotive Works, Winterthur

Stock
7 closed bogie coaches
1 bogie works car
1 4-wheel open wagon

Atmosphere at Llanberis as No 6 *Padarn* backs out towards the station. *C. C. Hall*

A source of a great many locomotives has been the South Wales scrapyard at Barry. Steam engines started leaving here for preservation almost as soon as BR finally eliminated steam working. Departure No 1 — LMS 0-6-0 No 43924 — left Barry for the Keighley & Worth Valley Railway in September 1968. The Mid-Hants Railway has provided a home for 12 former Barry locomotives, two, Nos 31806 and 34016 *Bodmin*, are seen here heading a Santa Special on 12 December 1981. At the time of writing a total of 147 have departed. *K. Livermore*

Talyllyn Railway

Headquarters: Talyllyn Railway Co, Wharf station, Tywyn, Gwynedd LL36 9EY
Telephone: Tywyn 710472
Timetable information: Tywyn 711297
Main station: Tywyn Wharf
Other public stations: Tywyn Pendre, Rhydyronen, Bryngl as, Dolgoch Falls, Abergynolwyn, Nant Gwernol
Car parks: Tywyn Wharf, Dolgoch, Abergynolwyn
Access by public transport: Tywyn BR station. Crosville bus services to Tywyn
Refreshment facilities: Tywyn Wharf, Dolgoch, Abergynolwyn
Souvenir shops: Tywyn Wharf, Abergynolwyn
Museum: Tywyn Wharf
Depot: Tywyn Pendre
Passenger trains: 2ft 3in gauge line Tywyn-Nant Gwernol
Length of line: $7\frac{1}{2}$ miles
Period of public operation: Daily early April to end of September. Limited (not daily) in October, Christmas and New Year
Facilities for disabled: No problem for casual visitors, advanced notice preferred for groups. Access to shop and cafeteria possible at Tywyn and Abergynolwyn. Disabled toilet facilities near Abergynolwyn. Access possible to lower floor of museum. Limited capacity for wheelchairs on trains
Special notes: Special parties and private charter trains by arrangement. Children under 5 years of age free.
Feature article reference: RW November 1982 p566

Locomotives

Name	*No*	*Builder*	*Type*	*Built*
Talyllyn	1	F/Jennings (42)	0-4-2ST	1865
Dolgoch	2	F/Jennings (63)	0-4-0WT	1866
Sir Haydn	3	Hughes (323)	0-4-2ST	1878
Edward Thomas	4	K/Stuart (4047)	0-4-2ST	1921
Midlander	5	R/Hornsby (200792)	4wDM	1940
Douglas	6	Barclay (1431)	0-4-0WT	1918
Irish Pete	7	Barclay (2263)	0-4-2T	1949
Merseysider	8	R/Hornsby (476108)	4wDH	1964
Alf	9	Hunslet (4136)	0-4-0DM	1950

Stock
13 4-wheel coaches/vans
10 bogie coaches
42 wagons

Narrow Gauge Museum, Tywyn

Name	*No*	*Builder*	*Type*	*Built*
Dot	—	B/Peacock (2817)	0-4-0ST	1887
*Pet**	—	LNWR	0-4-0ST	1865
Rough Pup	—	Hunslet (541)	0-4-0ST	1891
—	2	K/Stuart (721)	0-4-0WT	1902
Jubilee 1867	—	M/Wardle (1382)	0-4-0ST	1897
George Henry	—	de Winton	0-4-0T	1877
—	13	Spence	0-4-0T	1895
Nutty	—	Sentinel (7701)	0-4-0VB	1929

*On loan from National Railway Museum

Stock
Various wagons and miscellaneous equipment

Welsh Highland Railway

Location: Porthmadog, Gwynedd, adjacent to BR station
Operating society/organisation: Welsh Highland Light Railway (1964) Ltd, Gelert's Farm Works, Madoc Street West, Porthmadog, Gwynedd LL49 9DY
Telephone: Porthmadog (0766) 3402 (weekends and operating days)
Car park: At terminus
Access by public transport: Rail service to Porthmadog BR station. Festiniog Railway Harbour station. Crosville bus to Porthmadog
On site facilities: Shop at car park, refreshments available
Passenger trains: 1ft $11\frac{1}{2}$in gauge line. Porthmadog-Pen-y-Mount. Return journey time 25 minutes
Length of line: $\frac{3}{4}$-mile

A train on the Welsh Highland Railway.

Facilities for disabled: Disabled passengers can be accommodated without prior notice — except in parties
Special notes: 1984 service at weekends from Easter-30 September. Daily 26 May-3 June, 7 July-2 September; and bank holidays

Locomotives

Name	No	Builder	Type	Built
Moel Tryfan	—	Bagnall (2875)	0-4-2T	1948
—	—	Bagnall (3050)	0-4-2T	1953
Russell	—	Hunslet (901)	2-6-2T	1906
Pedemoura	—	O&K (10808)	0-6-0WT	1924
Karen	—	Peckett (2024)	0-4-2T	1942
Nantmor	—	O&K (9239)	0-6-0WT	1921
Glaslyn	1	R/Hornsby (297030)	4wDM	1952
Kinnerley	2	R/Hornsby (354068)	4wDM	1953
—	—	R/Hornsby	4wDM	1938
—	—	R/Hornsby	4wDM	1946
Cnicht	36	M/Rail (8703)	4wDM	1941
LBLR	9	M/Rail (9547)	4wDM	1950
Katherine	—	M/Rail (605363)	4wDM	1968
Pilkingtons No 4	—	M/Rail	4wDM	1959
Pilkingtons No 6	—	M/Rail	4wDM	1968
Felin Foel	—	Hunslet (6285)	4wDM	1968

Stock
A collection of rolling stock including bogie coaches and numerous service construction vehicles

Welshpool and Llanfair Railway

Headquarters: Welshpool & Llanfair Light Railway Preservation Co Ltd, Llanfair Caereinion station, Powys
Telephone: Llanfair Caereinion 810441
Main station: Llanfair Caereinion
Other public stations: Castle Caereinion, Sylfaen, Welshpool (Raven Square)
Car park: Llanfair Caereinion, Welshpool
Souvenir shops: Llanfair Caereinion
Depot: Llanfair Caereinion
Passenger trains: 2ft 6in gauge line Welshpool-Llanfair Caereinion (8 miles)
Period of public operation: Easter holiday and weekends to June. Daily June to September, weekends to early October.
Feature article reference: TI No 43 p5

Stock
1 Wickham trolley
7 W&LLR wagons
9 ex-Admiralty wagons
2 ex-Bowater wagons
5 ex-Zillertalbahn coaches
4 ex-Sierra Leone coaches
1 ex-Chattenden & Upnor coach

Locomotives

Name	No	Builder	Type	Built
The Earl	1	B/Peacock (3496)	0-6-0T	1902
The Countess	2	B/Peacock (3497)	0-6-0T	1902
—	5	Tubize (2369)	2-6-2T	1948
Monarch	6	Bagnall (3024)	0-4-4-0	1953
Chattenden	7	Drewry (2263)	0-6-0DM	1949
Dougal	8	Barclay (2207)	0-4-0T	1946
Sir Drefaldwyn	10	Franco-Belge (2855)	0-8-0T	1944
—	11	Hunslet (2251)	0-4-0DM	1940
Joan	12	K/Stuart (4404)	0-6-2T	1927
—	14	Hunslet (3815)	2-6-2T	1954

Early morning at Llanfair. *Joan* runs off shed before taking the first train of the day to Welshpool. *P. H. Groom*

Vale of Rheidol Narrow Gauge Steam Railway

Headquarters: Vale of Rheidol Narrow Gauge Steam Railway, BR Station, Aberystwyth, Dyfed
Telephone: Aberystwyth 612377
Main station: Aberystwyth

Locomotives

Name	No	Origin	Type	Built
Owain Glyndwr	7	GWR	2-6-2T	1923
Llywelyn	8	GWR	2-6-2T	1923
Prince of Wales	9	D/Metcalfe	2-6-2T	1902

Other public stations: Devil's Bridge, Rhiwfron, Rheidol Falls, Aberffrwd, Nantyronen, Capel Bangor, Glanrafon, Llanbadarn
Car parks: Aberystwyth, Devil's Bridge
Access by public transport: Aberystwyth BR station: and Crosville bus services to Aberystwyth
Refreshment facilities: Aberystwyth, Devil's Bridge
Souvenir shop: Devil's Bridge
Depot: Aberystwyth (not open to the public)
Passenger trains: 1ft $11\frac{1}{2}$in gauge line Aberystwyth-Devil's Bridge
Period of public operation: Daily Easter-end of October
Length of line: $11\frac{1}{2}$ miles
Special notes: Operated by British Rail
Feature article references: RW September 1983, p480

Stock
16 bogie coaches including one Vista coach
1 4-wheel baggage van
12 wagons for maintenance use
1 inspection trolley

No 9 *Prince of Wales* simmers at Devil's Bridge having just arrived from Aberystwyth, 2 May 1983. *C. C. Hall*

Big Pit Mining Museum

Location: Blaenavon, Gwent
Operating society/organisation: Big Pit (Blaenafon) Trust Ltd, Big Pit, Blaenavon, Gwent NP4 9XP
Telephone: 0495 790311
Car park: Adjacent to railway terminus at Big Pit
Access by public transport: Blaenavon-Brynmawr buses
On site facilities: Limited facilities at railway but refreshments and shop available at museum
Public opening: Summer 1983
Special notes: The railway forms part of the Big Pit mining complex and incorporates the former mineral/passenger lines running through Big Pit

Corris Railway Society Museum

Location: Off A487, opposite Braichgoch Hotel, five miles north of Machynlleth
Operating society: The Corris Railway Society, Corris Station Yard, Gwynedd (postal address: Corris, Machynlleth, Powys)
Car park: Adjacent
Access by public transport: Crosville bus (S13) — Aberystwyth-Machynlleth-Dolgellau, and 'Trawscambria' (stop at Braichgoch Hotel)
On site facilities: Toilets and children's playground
Public opening: Tuesday-Friday mid-July and August 13.30-17.30 and also on Bank Holiday weekends and other times as advertised locally

Locomotives

Name	*No*	*Builder*	*Type*	*Built*
Alan Meaden	5	M/rail (22258)	4wDM	1965
—	6	R/Hornsby (51849)	4wDM	1966

Stock
Small number of representative wagons. Gauge 2ft 3in

Conwy Valley Railway Museum

Location: Adjacent to Betws-y-Coed station
Operating society/organisation: Old Goods Yard, Betws-y-Coed, Gwynedd LL24 0AL
Telephone: (06902) 568
Car park: On site
Access by public transport: Betws-y-Coed BR station
On site facilities: Refreshments in buffet car, bookshop within the museum, miniature railway (7¼in gauge)
Public opening: Daily Easter to October. Summer and Bank Holiday weeks 10.30-17.30. Spring and Autumn 14.00-17.00
Facilities for disabled: Access to museum and toilets

Locomotives

Name	No	Builder	Type	Built
Sgt Murphy	—	K/Stuart (3117)	0-6-0T	1918

Stock
1 GWR fitter's van
1 LMS 6-wheel van
1 LNER CCT van
1 BR Mk 1 coach
2 SR luggage vans
1 Pullman coach
1 LNWR brake van

Narrow Gauge Railway Centre

Location: Off the A470 Blaenau Ffestiniog road ½ mile north of the town, turn at The Locomotive
Operating society/organisation: Narrow Gauge Enterprises, Gloddfa Ganol Mountain Tourist Centre, Blaenau Ffestiniog, Gwynedd, North Wales LL41 3NB
Telephone: Moelwyn (076 689) 500
Car park: On site
Access by public transport: Blaenau Ffestiniog BR/FR Station. Crosville bus connection
On site facilities: Licensed restaurant, snack bar and grill. Toilets, children's playground and playroom, slate works, craftshops, mining museum, preserved quarrymen's cottages, slate grotto and Land Rover tours
Public opening: Daily from Easter to October between 10.00 and 17.00. Coach parties welcome and educational parties catered for

Not all locomotives on display. Most locomotives have their works numbers painted on for identification

Locomotives

Name	No	Builder	Type	Built
Rail Taxi	—	BMW/Morris	4-2-0PMR	1967
—	—	BEV (551)	4wBE	1924
Welsh Pony	—	BEV (640)	4wE	1926
Dorothy	—	Bagnall (1568)	0-4-0ST	1899
—	—	Baguley (646)	0-4-0ParM	1917
—	—	Baguley (736)	0-4-0ParM	1918
—	—	Baguley (760)	0-4-0ParM	1918
Oakeley	—	Baguley (774)	0-4-0ParM	1919
The Wee Pug	—	Barclay (984)	0-4-0T	1903
Bredbury	3205	Bredbury UDC	4wPM	c1954
—	—	Brush (16303)	4wBE	1917
—	—	Brush (16306)	4wBE	1917
Kathleen	—	de Winton	0-4-0VBT	1877
Llanfair	—	de Winton	0-4-0VBT	1895
Spondon	—	D&NEP Co	4wBE	1926
Delta	—	Deutz (257081)	0-4-0DM	c1930
Festiniog	—	Festiniog Railway	4wDM	1974
—	—	Fowler (22900)	0-4-0DM	1941
—	—	Fowler (3930044)	4wDM	1950
—	—	Greenbat (1840)	4wBE	1942
—	—	Hibberd (1568)	4wPM	1927
—	—	Hibberd (1747)	4wPM	1931
—	—	Hibberd (1881)	4wPM	1934
—	—	Hibberd (2025)	4wDM	1937
—	—	Hibberd (2201)	4wDM	1939
—	—	Hibberd (3424)	4wPM	1949
—	—	Hibberd (4008)	4wDM	1963
—	—	Howard (982)	4wPM	1931
—	—	Hudson (36863)	4wDM	1929
—	—	Hudson (39924)	4wP/ParM	c1931
—	—	Hudson (45913)	4wP/ParM	1932
—	—	H/Clarke (D564)	4wDM	1930
—	—	Hunslet (1835)	4wDM	1937
—	—	Hunslet (2024)	4wDM	1940
Blaenau Ffestiniog	—	Hunslet (2207)	4wDM	1941
Dolwyddelan	—	Hunslet (2209)	4wDM	1941
—	—	Hunslet (2666)	4wDM	1942
—	—	Hunslet (6018)	4wDM	1961
—	—	K/Stuart (2442)	0-6-0T	1915

Name	No	Builder	Type	Built
—	—	K/Stuart (2451)	0-6-0T	1915
—	—	K/Stuart (3010)	0-6-0T	1916
—	—	K/Stuart (3014)	0-6-0T	1916
—	—	Lister (3916)	4wPM	1931
—	—	Lister (6299)	4wPM	1935
Whippit Quick	—	Lister (6502)	4w-4DMR	1935
Steam Tram	—	Lister (14005)	4wVBT	1970
—	C37	Locospoor (B7281E)	2-2wPM	—
—	2182	M/Rail (461)	4wPM	1917
—	—	M/Rail (22128)	4wDM	1962
—	—	M/Rail (105H006)	4wDH	1969
—	—	Muir Hill	4wP/ParM	1925
—	—	O&K (4470)	4wPM	c1931
—	LM11	Ruhrthaler (1082)	0-4-0DM	c1936
—	—	R/Hornsby (164346)	4wDM	1932
—	—	R/Hornsby (164350)	4wDM	1932
—	—	R/Hornsby (166028)	4wDM	1932
—	—	R/Hornsby (198297)	4wDM	1939
—	—	R/Hornsby (211647)	4wDM	1941
Pen-yr-Orsedd	—	R/Hornsby (235711)	4wDM	1945
—	—	R/Hornsby (393327)	4wDM	1956
—	—	R/Hornsby (398102)	4wDM	1956
—	ZM32	R/Hornsby (416214)	4wDM	1957
—	—	R/Hornsby (432664)	4wDM	1959
—	—	R/Proctor (50823)	4wParM	1915
Thakeham	—	Thakeham Tiles	4wPM	c1946
—	C13	Wickham (2449)	2w-2PMR	1938
—	—	Wickham (4091)	2w-2PMR	1946
—	—	Wickham (4092)	2w-2PMR	1946
—	TR27	Wickham (4132)	2w-2PMR	1947
—	TR8	Wickham (4151)	2w-2PMR	1948
—	TR10	Wickham (4162)	2w-2PMR	1948
—	TR12	Wickham (4165)	2w-2PMR	1948
—	TR41	Wickham (4168)	2w-2PMR	1948
—	C18	Wickham (4808)	2w-2PMR	1948
—	C20	Wickham (4810)	2w-2PMR	1948
—	C23	Wickham (4813)	2w-2PMR	1948
—	C26	Wickham (4816)	2w-2PMR	1948
Little George	—	Wingrove (1298)	0-4-0BE	1938

Penrhyn Castle Industrial Railway Museum

Location: Llandegai, near Bangor. One mile east of Bangor on the A5
Operating society/organisation: National Trust, Penrhyn Castle, Industrial Railway Museum, Llandegai, near Bangor, Gwynedd
Telephone: Bangor 53084
Car park: Within castle grounds
Access by public transport: Nearest BR station, Bangor
On site facilities: The castle is open to the public, and contains a gift shop. Light refreshments are available
Public opening: Daily 1 April-31 October
Facilities for disabled: Access to castle and museum
Special notes: For those interested in stately homes the castle is well worth a visit. The entrance fee covers both the castle and the railway exhibits housed in the castle courtyard

Industrial locomotives

Name	No	Builder	Type	Built
Kettering Furnaces No 3	—	B/Hawthorn (859)	0-4-0ST	1883
Watkin	—	de Winton	0-4-0VBT	1893
Fire Queen	—	Horlock	0-4-0	1848
Hawarden	—	H/Clarke (526)	0-4-0ST	1899
Vesta	—	H/Clarke (1223)	0-6-0T	1916
Charles	—	Hunslet (283)	0-4-0ST	1882
Hugh Napier	—	Hunslet (855)	0-4-0ST	1904
—	1	Neilson (1561)	0-4-0WT	1870
Haydock	—	Stephenson (2309)	0-6-0T	1879

Stock

7 narrow gauge rolling stock exhibits from the Padarn/Penrhyn system.
The small relics section includes a comprehensive display of railway signs.

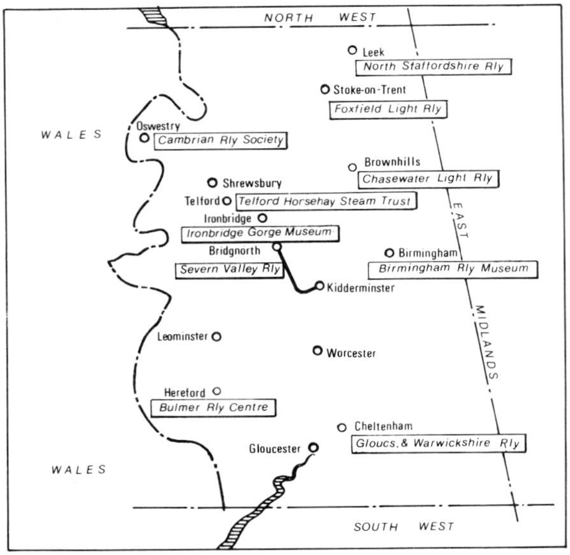

Severn Valley Railway

Headquarters: The Railway Station, Bewdley, Worcestershire
Telephone: Bewdley 403816
Main stations: Bridgnorth, Bewdley
Other public stations: Arley, Highley, Hampton Loade, Eardington, Northwood Halt
Car parks: At all stations
Access by public transport: Midland Red bus services Nos X92 to Bewdley, 890 to Bridgnorth
Refreshment facilities: Bridgnorth, Hampton Loade, Bewdley, Arley, Highley and on most trains
Souvenir shops: Bridgnorth, Bewdley, and Model Railway at Bewdley
Depot: Bridgnorth (locomotives), Bewdley (stock)
Passenger trains: Steam-hauled trains Bridgnorth-Bewdley, services proposed to be extended to Kidderminster from July 1984
Length of line: 12$\frac{1}{2}$ miles to Bewdley, will be 16 miles when Kidderminster is opened
Period of public operation: Weekends March-October and Santa Steam specials in late November and December. Daily service mid May to early September and all public bank holidays.
Facilities for disabled: Facilities available, special vehicle under conversion to carry wheelchairs
Special notes: A number of special enthusiasts' weekends and special events are held when extra trains are operated. In addition supplementary trains with diesel haulage may be run on special occasions
Feature article references: RW June 1982 p311; RW August 1982 p403 (diesels)

Locomotives

Name	No	Origin	Class	Type	Built
The Great Marquess	3442	LNER	K4	2-6-0	1938
Gordon	AD600	LMR	WD	2-10-0	1943
—	43106	LMS	4MT	2-6-0	1951
—	6443	LMS	2MT	2-6-0	1950
—	46521	LMS	2MT	2-6-0	1953
—	5000	LMS	5MT	4-6-0	1934
RAF Biggin Hill	45110	LMS	5MT	4-6-0	1935
Leander	5690	LMS	'Jubilee'	4-6-0	1936
—	47383	LMS	3F	0-6-0T	1926
Galatea	5699	LMS	'Jubilee'	4-6-0	1936
—	8233	LMS	8F	2-8-0	1940
—	2968	LMS	5P4F	2-6-0	1933
—	813	GWR	—	0-6-0ST	1901
—	3205	GWR	2251	0-6-0	1946
—	2857	GWR	2800	2-8-0	1918
—	5164	GWR	5101	2-6-2T	1930
—	4150	GWR	5101	2-6-2T	1947
—	4141	GWR	5101	2-6-2T	1946
—	5764	GWR	5700	0-6-0PT	1929
—	7714	GWR	5700	0-6-0PT	1930
Raveningham Hall	6960	GWR	'Hall'	4-6-0	1944
—	4566	GWR	4500	2-6-2T	1924
Bradley Manor	7802	GWR	'Manor'	4-6-0	1939
Hinton Manor	7819	GWR	'Manor'	4-6-0	1939
Erlestoke Manor	7812	GWR	'Manor'	4-6-0	1939
Hagley Hall	4930	GWR	'Hall'	4-6-0	1929
—	1501	GWR	1500	0-6-0PT	1949
—	9303	GWR	4300	2-6-0	1932
—	80079	BR	4MT	2-6-4T	1954
—	78019	BR	2MT	2-6-0	1954
—	75069	BR	4MT	4-6-0	1955
Western Ranger	D1013	BR	52	C-C	1962
Western Courier	D1062	BR	52	C-C	1963
—	D3022	BR	08	0-6-0	1952

Stock

27 ex-GWR coaches
13 ex-LMS coaches
14 ex-BR Mk 1 coaches
7 ex-LNER coaches
Numerous examples of ex-GWR, LMS and other freight vehicles and two 30-ton steam cranes

Industrial locomotives

Name	No	Builder	Type	Built
Shropshire	193	Hunslet (3793)	0-6-0ST	1953
—	4	Peckett (1738)	0-4-0ST	1928
Warwickshire	—	M/Wardle (2047)	0-6-0ST	1926
The Lady Armaghdale	—	Hunslet (686)	0-6-0T	1898
—	—	Ruston (319290)	0-4-0DM	1953
Alan	—	Ruston (11509)	0-4-0DM	1957
Archibald	—	Ruston (11510)	0-4-0DM	1957
William	—	Ruston (11512)	0-4-0DM	1957

Owners

3442 (the Viscount Garnock)
AD600 (the Ministry of Defence)
43106 (the Ivatt 4 Fund)
5000 (on loan from the National Railway Museum)
47383 (the Manchester Rail Travel Society)
8233 (the Stanier 8F Locomotive Society)
2968 (the Stanier Mogul Fund)
3205 (2251 Class Fund)
2857 (the 2857 Fund)
5164 (The 51XX Fund)
4150 (the 4150 Locomotive Fund)
4141 (the 4141 Fund)
5764, 7714 (the Pannier Tank Fund)
4566 (the 4566 Fund)
7802, 7812 (the Erlestoke Manor Fund)
7819 (the Hinton Manor Fund)
1501 (the 15XX Trust)
9303 (the Great Western (SVR) Association)
80079 (the Passenger Tank Fund)
75069 (the 75069 Fund)

Ivatt 4MT 2-6-0 No 43106 nears Northwood Halt in December 1982. *P. J. Green*

Foxfield Light Railway

Headquarters: Foxfield Light Railway, Dilhorne, Blythe Bridge, Stoke on Trent
Main station: Blythe Bridge (Caverswall Road)
Car park: Blythe Bridge
Access by public transport: BR Blythe Bridge (400yd). PMT bus service to Blythe Bridge
Refreshment facilities: Blythe Bridge
Souvenir shop: Blythe Bridge
Passenger trains: Steam-hauled trains operate from Blythe Bridge (Caverswall Road) to Dilhorne Park
Length of line: $2\frac{3}{4}$ miles
Period of public operation: Steam trains operate Sundays and Bank Holidays only, April-September between Blythe Bridge and Dilhorne Park. Museum open weekends throughout the year and afternoons daily April-September. Special trains at other times by prior arrangement
Facilities for disabled: Access to majority of facilities is on the level. For special requirements prior notice is desirable
Special notes: Wine and Dine Specials will operate on a number of Saturday evenings during the operating season.

Industrial locomotives

Name	No	Builder	Type	Built
Whiston	—	Hunslet (3694)	0-6-0ST	1950
Wimblebury	—	Hunslet (3839)	0-6-0ST	1956
Roker	—	RSH (7006)	0-4-0CT	1940
Rhiwnant	35	M/Wardle (1317)	0-6-0ST	1895
Robert	—	Avonside (2068)	0-6-0ST	1933
Cranford	—	Avonside (1919)	0-6-0ST	1924
Topham	—	Bagnall (2193)	0-6-0ST	1922
Lewisham	—	Bagnall (2221)	0-6-0ST	1927
Hawarden	—	Bagnall (2623)	0-4-0ST	1940
Little Barford	—	Barclay (2069)	0-4-0ST	1939
—	—	E/Electric (1130)	0-4-0BE	1939
Henry Cort	—	Peckett (933)	0-4-0ST	1903
Ironbridge No 3	—	Peckett (1803)	0-4-0ST	1933
—	11	Peckett (2081)	0-4-0ST	1947
—	1	Barclay (1984)	0-4-0F	1930
—	—	Simplex (2262)	4wDM	1924
Coronation	—	N/British (27097)	4wDH	1953
—	1	Peckett (1803)	0-4-0ST	1933
—	—	R/Hornsby (395305)	0-4-0DM	1956
Gas-oil	—	R/Hornsby	0-4-0DM	
Hercules	—	Ruston (242915)	4wDM	1946

Stock

3 coaches
4 scenery vans
19 wagons
1 steam crane

Birmingham Railway Museum

Location: 670 Warwick Road, Tyseley, Birmingham B11 2HL
Operating society/organisation: Birmingham Railway Museum Trust
Telephone: 021-707-4696
Car park: Site
Access by public transport: WMPTE bus routes Nos 37, 44 from city centre. BR service to Tyseley station
On site facilities: This former BR motive power depot has been equipped with much specialised railway engineering machinery. Souvenir shop, buffet, passenger demonstration line and station, schools education service
Length of line: $\frac{1}{4}$ mile
Public opening: Static display daily 10.00-17.00 except Christmas and New Year. Steam days on first Sunday of each month, and bank holidays, April-December 10.00-17.00
Special notes: Tyseley is a centre for 'Steam on BR' railtours over the BR lines to Stratford upon Avon and Didcot (via Oxford). Development plans envisage the construction of a roundhouse, small exhibits museum, and other ancillary features over the next 10 years financed by Local Authority grants. In 1983 an Education Service for schools began operating, providing a service of visits to schools in the Midlands and party visits from schools to the museum. Membership is available to the public at normal rates providing free entry to site events, magazines etc.
Feature article reference: RW June 1983 p302/306

Locomotives

Name	*No*	*Origin*	*Class*	*Type*	*Built*
Albert Hall	4983	GWR	'Hall'	4-6-0	1931
Earl of Mount Edgcumbe	5043	GWR	'Castle'	4-6-0	1936
Defiant	5080	GWR	'Castle'	4-6-0	1939
Thornbury Castle	7027	GWR	'Castle'	4-6-0	1949
Clun Castle	7029	GWR	'Castle'	4-6-0	1950
—	7752	GWR	5700	0-6-0PT	1930
—	7760	GWR	5700	0-6-0PT	1930
—	9600	GWR	5700	0-6-0PT	1945
Kolhapur	5593	LMS	'Jubilee'	4-6-0	1934

Industrial locomotives

Name	*No*	*Builder*	*Type*	*Built*
Rocket	—	Peckett (1722)	0-4-0ST	1926
—	1	Peckett (2004)	0-4-0ST	1942

Stock

1 Pullman car
1 Gresley buffet car
1 LNWR Royal Saloon
1 GWR semi Royal Saloon
1 30ton steam crane and sundry goods vehicles
1 GWR Inspection Saloon

Bulmer Railway Centre

Location: H. P. Bulmer Ltd (Cider Makers), Whitecross Road, Hereford. The site is $\frac{1}{4}$ mile from city centre on A438 Hereford-Brecon road
Operating society: The 6000 Locomotive Association in conjunction with the Merchant Navy Locomotive Preservation Society and the Princess Elizabeth Locomotive Society, on behalf of H. P. Bulmer Ltd
Telephone: Whitchurch (Avon) 834430
Car park: At the site
Access by public transport: Midland Red bus services and Yeoman's Hereford-Kington & Credenhill bus services. Hereford (BR) station (1 mile)
On site facilities: Sales. Refreshment facilities on steam days only

No 6000 *King George V* inside the locomotive shed.
D. R. Fitz-Gerald

Public opening: Weekends April-September. Telephone for details of special events and other information
Special notes: Hereford is a centre for 'Steam on BR' railtours over BR main lines
Feature article references: RW September 1982 p478; 35028 RW January 1983 p31; RW November 1983 p592 (locomotive 6201)

Locomotives

Name	No	Origin	Class	Type	Built
King George V	6000	GWR	'King'	4-6-0	1927
—	5786	GWR	5700	0-6-0PT	1930
Clan Line	35028	SR	MN	4-6-2	1948
Princess Elizabeth	6201	LMS	7P	4-6-2	1933
Cider Queen	2 (D2758)	Hunslet (6999)	05	0-6-0DH	1955

Industrial locomotives

Name	No	Builder	Type	Built
Pectin	—	Peckett (1579)	0-4-0ST	1921
Carnarvon	47	Kitson (5474)	0-6-0ST	1934

Stock
H. P. Bulmer 'Cider Train' consisting of five Pullman cars converted for exhibition purposes
Gresley Buffet coach
Several ex-BR Mk1 coaches
Pullman car from ex-SR 6-PUL electric unit
Small number of freight vehicles

Owners
6201 (the Princess Elizabeth Locomotive Society)
35028 (the Merchant Navy Locomotive Preservation Society)
6000 (on loan from the National Railway Museum/Borough of Thamesdown)

Cambrian Railways Society

Location: Oswestry station yard, Oswald Road, Oswestry, Shropshire
Operating society/organisation: Cambrian Railways Society Ltd, J. L. D. Price, 9 Liverpool Road West, Oswestry, Shropshire SY11 1PE
Car park: Station Road 100yd
Public opening: Sundays 11am-5pm

Stock
1 GWR auto-trailer
1 LMS brakevan
2 tank wagons
1 open wagon

Owners
7822 (the Foxcote Manor Society)

Locomotive

Name	No	Origin	Class	Type	Built
Foxcote Manor	7822	GWR	'Manor'	4-6-0	1950

Industrial locomotives

Name	No	Builder	Type	Built
—	1872	B/Peacock (1827)	0-4-0ST	1879
—	1	H/Clarke	0-4-0DM	1954
Adam	1	Peckett (1430)	0-4-0ST	1916
—	3	Hunslet (D843)	0-6-0DM	1954
—	6	Peckett (2131)	0-4-0ST	1951
—	8	A/Barclay (885)	0-6-0ST	1900
—	322	Planet (3541)	4wDM	1952
Norma	3770	Hunslet (3770)	0-6-0ST	1952

Chasewater Light Railway

Location: Chasewater Pleasure Park, Brownhills, West Midlands
Operating society/organisation: Chasewater Light Railway Society
Telephone: 021 355 3812 (Hon Sec) Brownhills 375852 (railway)
Car park: Pleasure park
Access by public transport: Midland Red bus services Nos 154 and 156 from Birmingham and Cannock, Nos 345 and 394 from Walsall

Sentinel (9632) shunting at the main depot. *A. Pearson*

On site facilities: Refreshments, museum and souvenir shop. Extensive small relics collection
Public opening: Extensive track reorganisation may mean no trains run during 1984.
Site open 2pm-dusk Saturday and Sundays throughout the year

Industrial locomotives

Name	No	Builder	Type	Built
—	—	Peckett (917)	0-4-0ST	1902
—	—	Barclay (2220)	0-4-0ST	1946
—	—	Barclay (1223)	0-4-0ST	1911
The Colonel	—	Peckett (1351)	0-4-0ST	1914
Alfred Paget	11	Neilson (2937)	0-4-0ST	1882
—	S100	H/Clarke (1822)	0-6-0T	1949
—	15	H/Clarke (431)	0-6-0ST	1895
Asbestos	—	H/Leslie (2780)	0-4-0ST	1909
—	20	Kent/Planet	4wDM	1926
—	21	Kent/Planet (1612)	4wDM	1929
—	DL7	R/Hornsby	0-4-0DE	1961
—	—	Smiths	4wD crane	1951
—	—	Sentinel (9632)	4wVBT	1957

Stock
Passenger services provided with ex-BR dmu trailer cars.
A selection of freight vehicles is also housed at the site, also several pre-Grouping coaches.

Dean Forest Railway

Location: Norchard Steam Centre on the B4234, ½-mile off A48 at Lydney, Glos
Operating society/organisation: Dean Forest Railway Society in conjunction with owning company, Forest of Dean Railway Ltd
Telephone: Dean (0594) 43423
Car park: Adequate for cars and coaches — no charge
Access by public transport: B4234 from Lydney. National Welsh bus service No 24 passes the site
On site facilities: A shop and refreshments are available at Norchard along with a small museum
Public opening: Daily for static display — shop, museum, refreshments open every Saturday and Sunday 11.00-17.00 and weekdays July and August. Steam days 1984: Every bank holiday Sunday and Monday, 8 April, 26/27 June, each Sunday June-September, 21 October, 9/16 December. (26/27 June are Schools Days, 8 July Enthusiasts Day, 21 October Vintage Vehicle Day, 9/16 December Santa Specials)
Length of line: ⅔-mile
Facilities for disabled: Access to coaches, museum, refreshment bar. Toilets
Special notes: Steam rides to Middle Forge (⅔ mile) from Norchard. Depending on LRO application, the service may be extended on to part of the Lydney-Parkend line when purchase completed and track brought up to necessary standard

Stock
7 ex-GWR coaches
10 ex-BR coaches
2 Wickham trolleys
1 steam crane Thos Smith (Rodley) No TS 5027
50+ wagons

Locomotives

Name	No	Origin	Class	Type	Built
—	229	GER	209	0-4-0ST	1876
—	4121	GWR	5101	2-6-2T	1937
—	5521	GWR	4575	2-6-2T	1928
—	5532*	GWR	4575	2-6-2T	1928
—	5541	GWR	4575	2-6-2T	1928
—	9681	GWR	5700	0-6-0PT	1949
—	03.062	BR	03	0-6-0DM	1958

*For spares only

Industrial locomotives

Name	No	Builder	Type	Built
Jessie	—	Hunslet (1873)	0-6-0ST	1937
—	—	Fowler (4210101)	0-4-0DM	1955
G. B. Keeling	—	Hunslet (3806)	0-6-0ST	1953
—	—	Hunslet (2145)	0-4-0DM	1940
Uskmouth No 1	—	Peckett (2147)	0-4-0ST	1952
—	—	Hibberd (3947)	4wPM	1960
—	39	R/Royce (10218)	0-6-0DH	1965

Hunslet 0-6-0ST *G. B. Keeling* on passenger duty passes some of the line's rolling stock on its way back to Norchard.

Gloucester Warwickshire Railway

Location: Toddington Station, Toddington
Operating society/organisation: Gloucester Warwickshire Steam Railway PLC, The Station, Toddington, Cheltenham, Glos GL54 5DT
Telephone: Winchcombe 602946
Access by public transport: NBC service X68 between Stratford and Gloucester (Sunday-Friday). Also Marchant Coaches and Castleway Coaches from Cheltenham, Cresswell Coaches from Evesham and Blockley. Public transport is very limited
On site facilities: Sales, catering, museum, narrow gauge rides, toilets
Public opening: Weekends and Bank Holidays, 10.00-17.00. During the week the station is unmanned but visitors are welcome
Car park: On site
Special notes: The site is being developed at the headquarters of the railway between Cheltenham and Stratford. Application has been made for an LRO between Cheltenham and Broadway, the granting of which will allow the purchase of this section. The first length of operating railway will be between Toddington and Winchombe. A number of special events are organised during the year
Feature article references: TI No 41 p8; TI No 45 p20

Stock
9 ex-GWR coaches
6 ex-BR coaches
1 ex-LMS coach
30 wagons

Owners
2807 (the Cotswold Locomotive Preservation Ltd)
7821 (the GW Steam Locomotive Group)
7828 (the GW Steam Locomotive Group)
5952 (the GW Steam Locomotive Group)
35006 (the P and O Locomotive Society)
D9537 and D9539 (Cotswold Diesel Preservation Society)

Locomotives

Name	*No*	*Origin*	*Class*	*Type*	*Built*
—	2807	GWR	2800	2-8-0	1905
Cogan Hall	5952	GWR	'Hall'	4-6-0	1935
Ditcheat Manor	7821	GWR	'Manor'	4-6-0	1950
Odney Manor	7828	GWR	'Manor'	4-6-0	1950
Peninsular and Oriental SNCo	35006	SR	MN	4-6-2	1941
—	D9537	BR	14	0-6-0DH	1965
—	D9539	BR	14	0-6-0DM	1965

Industrial locomotives

Name	*No*	*Builder*	*Type*	*Built*
—	1	Avonside (1977)	0-4-0T	1925
—	2	A/Barclay (2221)	0-4-0ST	1946
John	—	Peckett (1976)	0-4-0ST	1939
Drake	—	A/Barclay (2086)	0-4-0ST	1940
—	—	A/Barclay (2126)	0-4-0F	1940
King George	—	Hunslet (2409)	0-6-0ST	1942
—	19	Fowler (4240016)	0-6-0DH	1964
—	21	Fowler (4210130)	0-4-0DM	1957
—	—	H/Clarke (D615)	0-6-0DM	1938
—	—	Hibberd (2893)	4wP	1943

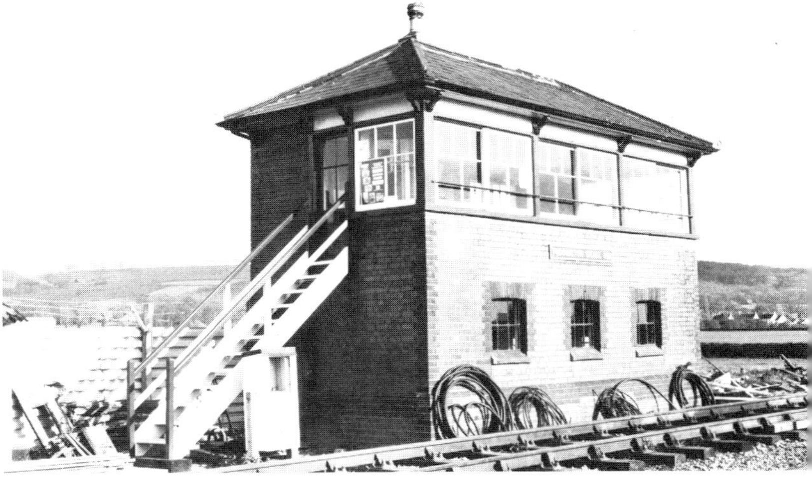

The restored signalbox at Toddington.
P. Nicholson

Industrial narrow gauge locomotives

Name	*No*	*Builder*	*Type*	*Built*
George B	—	Hunslet (680)	0-4-0ST	1898
Chaka	—	Hunslet	0-4-2T	1940
Justine	—	Jung (939)	0-4-0WT	1906
—	2	Lister (34523)	4wDM	1949
—	3	M/Rail (4565)	4wPM	1928
Spitfire	—	M/Rail (7053)	4wPM	1937
—	1	R/Hornsby (166010)	4wDM	1932
—	L5	R/Hornsby (18120)	4wDM	1936
—	—	R/Hornsby (354028)	4wDM	1953

Stock
1 coach
11 wagons

North Staffordshire Railway

Location: Cheddleton station, near Leek, Staffordshire
Operating society/organisation: North Staffordshire Railway Company (1978) Ltd
Telephone: Stoke on Trent 48544 (evenings), Churnet Side 360522 (9.00-17.00)
Car park: At the station
Access by public transport: A regular bus service operated by Proctors and Berresfords, from the Potteries, Hanley and Leek to Cheddleton village
On site facilities: Include a museum, sales area, toilets and refreshment rooms
Public opening: Easter-September, Monday-Friday 12.00-16.30. Sundays and bank holidays 11.30-18.00. October-April Sundays only 11.30-dusk. Closed Saturdays and Christmas Day

Locomotives

Name	*No*	*Origin*	*Class*	*Type*	*Built*
—	4422	LMS	4F	0-6-0	1927
—	80136	BR	4MT	2-6-4T	1956

Industrial locomotives

Name	*No*	*Builder*	*Type*	*Built*
Josiah Wedgwood	3777	Hunslet (3777)	0-6-0ST	1952
Camel	—	RSH (6980)	0-4-0DM	1940

Special notes: Facilities for the disabled. Coach parties and charter trains by arrangement. Steam hauled passenger trains over 300yd line on frequent summer Sundays and bank holidays. 'Knotty' signalbox open on Sundays only

Stock
4 ex-BR Mk1 coaches
Several freight vehicles
1 diesel rail mounted crane

Telford Horsehay Steam Trust

Location: Horsehay, Telford, Shropshire
Operating society/organisation: Telford Horsehay Steam Trust, The Old Loco Shed, Horsehay, Telford, TF4 2LT
Public opening: Tuesday 19.00-22.00, Thursday 19.00-22.00, Saturday 10.00-17.00, Sunday 10.00-13.00. Parties may be accomodated at other times by arrangement with the secretary at the above address. Public steamings take place irregularly and are noted in the railway press
Feature article reference: TI No 46 p20

Stock
1 ex-BR Mk 1 coach
1 ex-GWR auto-trailer
1 Wickham trolley
Various wagons

Locomotives

Name	*No*	*Origin*	*Class*	*Type*	*Date*
—	5619	GWR	5600	0-6-2T	1925

Industrial locomotives

Name	*No*	*Builder*	*Type*	*Date*
Peter	—	A/Barclay (782)	0-6-0ST	1896
Tom	—	N/British (27414)	0-4-0DH	1954
—	—	Sentinel (9535)	4wVBT	1952
—	VL6	R/Hornsby (382824)	4wDM	1955
—	—	R/Hornsby (513141)	4wDM	1966

Ironbridge Gorge Museum

Location: Ironbridge, Shropshire
Operating society/organisation: Ironbridge Gorge Museum Trust, Ironbridge, Telford, Shropshire TF8 7AW

Locomotives

Name	*No*	*Origin*	*Class*	*Type*	*Built*
—	9395	LNWR	G2	0-8-0	1921†

No 9395, former LNWR 0-8-0 is on display at Blists Hill Open Air Museum.
A. Baker

Telephone: Ironbridge (095 245) 3522
Car park: At the site
Access by public transport: Midland Red bus services to Ironbridge
Public opening: Daily (10.00-18.00) April-October. Daily (10.00-17.00) November-March. Closed Christmas Day
Special notes: Tickets to the various museums are available
Feature article reference: TI No 46 p20

Locomotives

Name	*No*	*Builder*	*Type*	*Date*
—	—	Sentinel/Coalbrookdale (6185)	0-4-0VBT	1925*
—	—	Sentinel/M/Wardle (6155)	0-4-0VBT	1925*
—	5	Coalbrookdale	0-4-0ST	1865*

*At Museum of Iron, Coalbrookdale
†At Blists Hill Open Air Museum

Owners
485 (on loan from the National Railway Museum

Winchcombe Railway Museum

Location: 23 Gloucester Street, Winchcombe, Gloucestershire
Operating society/organisation: Winchombe Railway Museum Association, 23 Gloucester Street, Winchcombe, Gloucestershire
Telephone: Winchcombe (0242) 602257
Car park: On street at entrance
Access by public transport: Bus service from Cheltenham operated by Castleways Ltd
On site facilities: Relic and souvenir shop
Public opening: Easter, Mayday, Spring and Summer Bank Holiday Sunday and Monday
Sundays in July and August, Daily 7-14 August 14.30-18.00
Facilities for disabled: Access to all parts except toilets
Special notes: The museum specialises in signalling equipment, lineside fixtures, horse-drawn road vehicles, tickets, lamps etc. Indoor and outdoor displays

EAST MIDLANDS

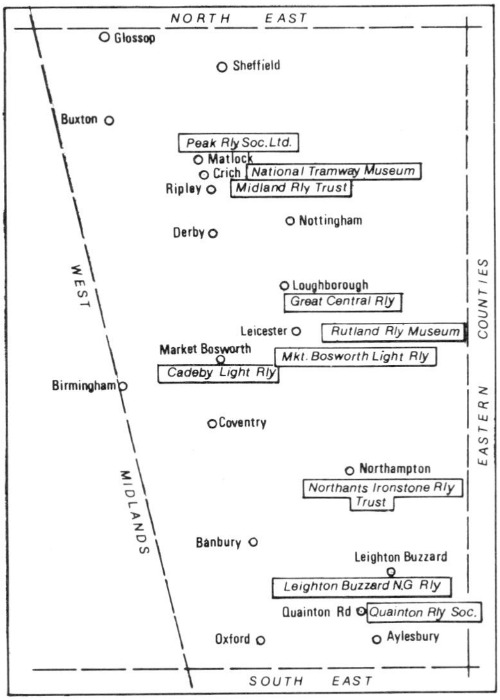

Great Central Railway

Headquarters: Great Central Railway, (1976) PLC (Main Line Steam Trust Ltd), Loughborough Central station, Great Central Road, Loughborough, Leicestershire LE11 1SS
Telephone: Loughborough 230726
Main station: Loughborough Central
Other public stations: Quorn & Woodhouse, Rothley
Car park: Quorn

Former Great Central Railway No 506 *Butler Henderson* pulls into Quorn & Woodhouse station on 25 June 1983. *A. C. Butcher*

Access by public transport: Loughborough BR station (¾ mile). Trent, South Notts & Midland Red bus services to Loughborough bus station (¾ mile)
Refreshment facilities: Buffet car and light refreshments on most trains. Lunches on midday trains Saturday and Sunday. Dinner trains run on Saturday nights, please contact railway for dates and reservations (advance booking only). Refreshment buffets at Loughborough and Rothley
Souvenir shop: Loughborough
Museum: Loughborough
Depot: Loughborough Central
Passenger trains: Loughborough-Rothley
Length of line: 5½ miles
Period of public operation: Weekends throughout the year and Bank Holidays, Wednesdays June, July and August
Facilities for disabled: Special carriage for wheelchair/disabled persons (advance notice required). Toilet facilities at all stations. Wheelchair access good at Quorn and Rothley, can be arranged at Loughborough with advance notification

Locomotives

Name	*No*	*Origin*	*Class*	*Type*	*Built*
Butler Henderson	506	GCR	'Director'	4-4-0	1919
—	68088	NER	Y7	0-4-0T	1923
—	5224	GWR	4200	2-8-0T	1924
Witherslack Hall	6990	GWR	'Hall'	4-6-0	1948
*	5231	LMS	5MT	4-6-0	1936
—	1264	LNER	B1	4-6-0	1947
Mayflower	1306	LNER	B1	4-6-0	1948
—	4744	LNER	N2	0-6-2T	1921
Boscastle	34039	SR	WC	4-6-2	1946
Duke of Gloucester	71000	BR	8P	4-6-2	1954
—	92212	BR	9F	2-10-0	1959
—	D4067	BR	10	0-6-0DM	1955
—	D9516	BR	14	0-6-0DH	1965
—	D9523	BR	14	0-6-0DH	1965

*No 5231 is named *3rd (Volunteer) Battalion The Worcestershire and Sherwood Foresters Regiment*

Industrial locomotives

Name	*No*	*Builder*	*Type*	*Built*
Marston No 3	—	H/Leslie (3581)	0-4-0ST	1924
—	7597	Hawthorns (7597)	0-6-0T	1949
—	9	Hunslet (3827)	0-6-0ST	1954
Robert Nelson	4	Hunslet (1800)	0-6-0ST	1936
Hilda	—	Peckett (1963)	0-4-0ST	1938
Qwag	1	Ruston (371971)	4wDM	1954
Arthur Wright	D4279	Fowler (4210079)	0-4-0DM	1952
Alen Grice	11	Sentinel	0-4-0D	1963

Owners
506 (on loan from the National Railway Museum)
68088 (the Y7 Locomotive Society)
4744 (the Gresley Society)
6990 (the Witherslack Hall Locomotive Society)
61264 (the Thompson B1 Locomotive Society)
71000 (the Duke of Gloucester Steam Locomotive Trust)
92212 (the 92212 Holdings Ltd)

Feature article reference: RW January 1982 p22

Market Bosworth Light Railway

Headquarters: Market Bosworth Light Railway, Shackerstone station, near Market Bosworth, Leicestershire
Telephone: 021 7861175 (administration only). 0827 880754 (weekends only)
Main station: Shackerstone
Other public station: Market Bosworth
Car park: Shackerstone
Access by public transport: Gibson Bros bus Leicester (Horsefair St) to Market Bosworth (square) weekdays and Sundays
Refreshment facilities: Shackerstone
Souvenir shop: Shackerstone
Museum: Shackerstone
Depot: Shackerstone

Locomotives

Name	*No*	*Origin*	*Class*	*Type*	*Built*
—	D2245	BR	04	0-6-0DM	1956

Industrial locomotives

Name	*No*	*Builder*	*Type*	*Built*
—	—	Bagnall (2648)	0-4-0ST	1941
The King	—	Borrows (48)	0-4-0WT	1906
—	11	Hunslet (1493)	0-4-0ST	1925
Dunlop No 7	—	Peckett (2130)	0-4-0ST	1951
—	3	RSH (7537)	0-6-0T	1949
—	4	RSH (7684)	0-6-0T	1951
Lamport No 3	—	Bagnall (2670)	0-6-0ST	1942

Passenger trains: Shackerstone-Market Bosworth
Length of line: 2¾ miles
Period of public operation: Easter Sunday and every Sunday and Bank Holiday Monday to 7 October 1984
Special notes: Market Bosworth Light Railway is operated by members of Shackerstone Railway Society Ltd. An extension of the line from Market Bosworth to Shenton and the battlefield of Bosworth is being undertaken

Name	*No*	*Builder*	*Type*	*Built*
Florence	2	Bagnall (3059)	0-6-0ST	1953
—	—*	R/Hornsby (235513)	4wDM	1945
The 1211 Squadron	—	R/Hornsby (347747)	0-6-0DM	1957
—	—	R/Hornsby (393304)	4wDM	1956
—	—	S/Crossley (7697)	0-6-0DM	1953

*Converted to steam power 1983

Stock
3 ex-BR Mk1 coaches
2 ex-BR converted dmu coaches
3 parcels vans
2 rail mounted steam cranes
1 rail mounted diesel crane
Small number of wagons
ex-BR Griddle car

Midland Railway Centre

Location: Midland Railway Centre, Butterley station, near Ripley, Derbyshire
Operating society/organisation: Midland Railway Trust Ltd
Telephone: Ripley 44920
Car park: Butterley station on A61 1 mile north of Ripley
On site facilities: Refreshments, souvenir shop, display vehicles and exhibition coach
Public opening: Every Saturday and Sunday from March-October, 10.00-dusk. Also open on Bank Holiday Mondays, and Wednesdays 4 July-29 August. Site open for static display April-September, Monday-Friday 10.00-17.00. Weekends only for static display November-February. All other times by arrangement
Length of line: 3 miles
Facilities for disabled: Toilets, special coach, access to shop but not cafeteria
Special notes: This centre is being established as a working museum of Midland and LMS Railway practice, which will eventually include a double track running line with stations built in original style.
Feature article reference: RW December 1982 p631

Stock
Numerous carriages and wagons

Locomotives

Name	*No*	*Origin*	*Class*	*Type*	*Built*
—	73129	BR	5MT	4-6-0	1956
Princess Margaret Rose	6203	LMS	8P	4-6-2	1936
—	4027	LMS	4F	0-6-0	1924
—	47564	LMS	3F	0-6-0T	1928
—	47327	LMS	3F	0-6-0T	1926
—	16440	LMS	3F	0-6-0T	1926
—	47445	LMS	3F	0-6-0T	1927
—	158A	MR	—	2-4-0	1866
—	1708	MR	1F	0-6-0T	1880
—	12077	BR	11	0-6-0DE	1950
—	13809	S&DJR	7F	2-8-0	1925
Great Gable	D4	BR	44	1Co-Co1	1959

Industrial locomotives

Name	*No*	*Builder*	*Type*	*Built*
Gladys	—	Markham (109)	0-4-0ST	1894
Stanton	24	Barclay (1875)	0-4-0CT	1925
—	68012	Hunslet (3193)	0-6-0ST	1944
Victory	—	Peckett (1547)	0-4-0ST	1917
—	4	N/Wilson (454)	0-4-0ST	1894
—	—	Sentinel (9370)	4wVBT	1947
Andy	—	Fowler (16038)	0-4-0DM	1923
*Handyman**	—	H/Clarke (573)	0-4-0ST	1900
—	RS9	M/Rail (2024)	0-4-0DM	1921
—	RS12	M/Rail (460)	0-4-0DM	1912
—	—	M/Rail (1930)	0-4-0PM	1919
—*	2	Fowler (20685)	2-4-0DM	1935
—	2	A/Barclay (2008)	0-4-0F	1935
—	D2959	R/Hornsby (384139)	0-4-0DE	1955

Owners
158A, 4027 (on loan from the National Railway Museum)
6203 (Butlins)
1708 (the 1708 Locomotive Preservation Trust)
13809 (the 13809 Preservation Group)
16440, 47327, 7445, 47564, 73129 (Derby City Council)

*3ft gauge

LMS 0-6-0T No 16440 crosses Butterley reservoir at the head of a Santa Special. *Midland Railway Trust*

Quainton Railway Centre

Location: Adjacent to BR goods only line to Aylesbury. Six miles north of Aylesbury. Turn off A41 at Waddesdon 6 miles NW of Aylesbury, Bucks

Operating society/organisation: Quainton Railway Society Ltd, The Railway Station, Quainton, near Aylesbury, Bucks HP22 4BY

Telephone: Quainton (029675) 450

Car park: Quainton Road — Free parking

Access by public transport: BR Aylesbury station, (charter shuttle service to Centre on bank holiday Mondays only). Red Rover Bus (tel 0296-28686 for details)

On site facilities: Souvenir bookshop, light refreshments, toilets, steam hauled train rides. Museum of small relics

Public opening: Every Sunday, 25 March to end of October. Engines only in steam on advertised open days, bank holiday Sundays and Mondays, last Sunday in each month, every Sunday in August. 10.00-18.00 on all dates

Length of line: $\frac{3}{4}$-mile demonstration track

Facilities for disabled: Access to most of site, but not toilets. No advance notice required

Special notes: OS Map reference SP738190. The largest collection of standard gauge locomotives, together with a most interesting collection of vintage coaching stock much of which was built in the last century

Feature article reference: RW August 1983 p404; TI No 44 p20

Locomotives

Name	*No*	*Origin*	*Class*	*Type*	*Built*
—	1	Met Rly		0-4-4T	1898
—	0314	LSWR	0298	2-4-0WT	1874
King Edward 1	6024	GWR	'King'	4-6-0	1930
Wightwick Hall	6989	GWR	'Hall'	4-6-0	1948
—	7200	GWR	7200	2-8-2T	1934
—	7715	GWR	5700	0-6-0PT	1930
—	9466	GWR	9400	0-6-0PT	1952
—	41298	LMS	2MT	2-6-2T	1951
—	41313	LMS	2MT	2-6-2T	1952
—	46447	LMS	2MT	2-6-0	1950
—	D2298	BR	04	0-6-0DM	1960

Industrial locomotives

Name	*No*	*Builder*	*Type*	*Built*
Sydenham	—	A/Porter (3567)	4wTG	1895
Scott	—	Bagnall (2469)	0-4-0ST	1932
Swanscombe	—	Barclay (699)	0-4-0ST	1891
Punch Hull	—	Barclay (776)	0-4-0ST	1896
Alexander	—	Barclay (1865)	0-4-0ST	1926
Tom Parry	—	Barclay (2015)	0-4-0ST	1935
GF3	—	Barclay (1477)	0-4-0F	1916
Swordfish	—	Barclay (2138)	0-6-0ST	1941
Laporte	—	Barclay (2243)	0-4-0F	1948
Osram	—	Fowler (20067)	0-4-0DM	1933
—	3	H/Leslie (3717)	0-4-0ST	1928
Sir Thomas	—	H/Clarke (1334)	0-6-0T	1918
Millom	—	H/Clarke (1742)	0-4-0ST	1946
Trym	—	Hunslet (287)	0-4-0ST	1882
Esso	—	Hunslet (2067)	0-4-0DM	194[illegible]
Arthur	—	Hunslet (3782)	0-6-0ST	1953
Juno	—	Hunslet (3850)	0-6-0ST	1958
—	65	Hunslet (3889)	0-6-0ST	1964
—	66	Hunslet (3890)	0-6-0ST	1964
Redland	—	K/Stuart (K4428)	0-4-0DM	1929
Coventry No 1	—	NBL (24564)	0-6-0ST	1939
Hornpipe	—	Peckett (1756)	0-4-0ST	1928
—	—	Peckett (1900)	0-4-0T	1936
—	—	Peckett (2104)	0-4-0ST	1948
—	—	Peckett (2105)	0-4-0ST	1948
—	T1	Hibberd (2102)	4wD	1937
Tarmac	—	Hibberd (3765)	0-4-0DM	1955
—	—	Sentinel (6515)	4wVBTG	1926
—	11	Sentinel (9366)	4wVBTG	1945
—	7	Sentinel (9376)	4wVBTG	1947
Chislet	9	Yorkshire (2498)	0-6-0ST	1951

***Coventry No 1* in action during an Industrial Steam Day.** *M. Ricks*

Owners
6024 (the 6024 Preservation Society Ltd)
41298 (the Ivatt Locomotive Trust)
41313 (the Ivatt Locomotive Trust)
46447 (the Ivatt Locomotive Trust)
9466 (the 9466 Group)
Juno (the Ivatt Locomotive Trust)

Stock
3 ex-BR Mk1 coaches
10 LNWR and 4 LMSR coaches
3 GCR, 2 GNR, 2 GWR, 1 LCDR and 3 LNER coaches
41 box vans, open wagons and miscellaneous vehicles
1 ex-London Underground carriage No 54233
1 2ft gauge Post Office Railway loco No 803

Peak Railway Society Ltd

Locations: Matlock Railway Station, Matlock, Derbyshire
Buxton Midland Station Site, Buxton, Derbyshire
Operating society/organisation: Peak Railway Society Ltd, Matlock Railway Station, Matlock, Derbyshire
Car parks: On site
Access by public transport: BR dmu service between Derby and Matlock on Mondays to Saturdays and between Manchester Piccadilly and Buxton daily
On site facilities: Shops at Matlock and Buxton, toilets and tearooms at Matlock
Public opening: Free access to sites at most times. Matlock and Buxton shops open weekends and summer weekdays. Also weekdays throughout the year at Matlock. It is planned to start brake van rides at Buxton in 1984 at which time a small charge may be made for site entrance
Special notes: Peak Rail (Operations) Ltd, has outline planning permission to relay the 20-mile line from Buxton to Matlock
Feature article reference: RW February 1983 p68

Locomotives

Name	*No*	*Origin*	*Class*	*Type*	*Built*
‡*Kinlet Hall*	4936	GWR	'Hall'	4-6-0	1929
**Hartland*	34101	SR	WC	4-6-2	1950
—	48624†	LMS	8F	2-8-0	1943
—	76084**	BR	4MT	2-6-0	1954
—	92214†	BR	9F	2-10-0	1959
—	80080‡	BR	4MT	2-6-4T	1954
—	80098††	BR	4MT	2-6-4T	1954

*In store Derby, under restoration
†At Buxton
‡At Matlock
**In store at Retford, under restoration
††Yet to arrive

Track laying in progress at Matlock, GWR No 4936 *Kinlet Hall* is in the bay platform.
D. & S. E. Barratt

Leighton Buzzard Narrow Gauge Railway

Headquarters: Leighton Buzzard Narrow Gauge Railway, Page's Park station, Billington Road, Leighton Buzzard LU7 8TN
Telephone: (0525) 373888
Main station: Pages Park, (Billington Road, Leighton Buzzard)
Other public stations: Halts at Vandyke Road and Stonehenge Works
Car park: Pages Park

Locomotives

Name	*No*	*Builder*	*Type*	*Built*
Chaloner	1*	de Winton	0-4-0VBT	1877
Pixie	2	K/Stuart (4260)	0-4-0ST	1922
Rishra	3	Baguley (2007)	0-4-0T	1921
The Doll	4	Barclay (1641)	0-6-0T	1919
Pam	7	O&K (8986)	4wDM	1939
Elf	5	O&K (12740)	0-6-0WT	1936

Orenstein & Koppel 0-6-0WT *Elf* provides the motive power early in 1983. *A. C. Butcher*

Access by public transport: Leighton Buzzard BR station then by bus to town centre
Refreshment facilities: Pages Park
Souvenir shop: Pages Park
Depots: Pages Park and Stonehenge Works
Passenger trains: 2ft gauge line Pages Park-Stonehenge Works
Length of line: 3 miles
Period of public operation: Sundays April-September and Bank Holiday Mondays (except Christmas), Wednesdays 1, 8, 15, 22 August
Facilities for disabled: Access to shop, buffet, platform. Toilet facilities are not specially available, Wheelchairs cannot be conveyed on trains although those persons who can be transferred from chair to train are conveyed by first available train
Feature article references: RW February 1982 p73

Name	No	Builder	Type	Built
Haydn Taylor	10	Simplex (7956)	4wDM	1945
P. C. Allen	11	O&K (5834)	0-4-0WT	1912
Carbon	12	Simplex (6012)	4wDM	1930
Caravan	6	Simplex (7192)	4wDM	1938
—	14	Hunslet (3646)	4wDM	1946
Tom Bombaldi	15	Planet (2514)	4wDM	1935
Thorin Oakenshield	16	Lister (11221)	4wDM	1939
Fëanor	22	M/Rail (11003)	4wDM	1954
—	23	M/Rail (11298)	4wDM	1965
—	25	M/Rail (60s317)	4wDM	1966
—	36	M/Rail (7214)	4wDM	1938
—	43	Simplex (10409)	4wDM	1954
Kestrel	44	Simplex (7933)	4wDM	1941

Stock
8 coaches and a number of miscellaneous vehicles

*No 1 is on loan to the National Railway Museum, York, due to return early 1984

Cadeby Light Railway

Location: One mile south of Market Bosworth on A447
Operating society/organisation: The Rev E. R. Boston, Cadeby Rectory, Cadeby, Nuneaton, Warwicks
Telephone: Market Bosworth 290462
Car park: In local side roads
Access by public transport: Midland Red, 678 from Hinckley, Leicester Corp/Gibson Bros (Comfort Coaches) 124
On site facilities: 2ft gauge railway, also traction engines and a model railway
Public opening: Second Saturday of each month

Stock
Penrhyn Quarrymans coach
2 fullersite wagons
2 flat trucks
7 open trucks
2 platelayers trolleys

Locomotives

Name	No	Builder	Type	Built
Pixie	1	Bagnall (2090)	0-4-0ST	1919
Margaret	—	Hunslet (605)	0-4-0ST	1894
—	2	O&K (7529)	0-4-0WT	1914
—	2	Bagulay (1695)	0-4-0PM	1928
New Star	—	Lister (4088)	4wPM	1931
—	20	M/Rail (8748)	4wDM	1942
—	42	M/Rail (7710)	4wDM	1939
—	87004	M/Rail (2197)	4wDM	1922
—	—	M/Rail (4572)	4wDM	1929
—	—	M/Rail (5609)	4wDM	1931
—	24	M/Rail (5853)	4wDM	1934
—	—	H/Clarke (D558)	4wDM	1930
—	—	R/Hornsby (179870)	4wDM	1936

***Pixie* in action on the Cadeby Light Railway.** *A. Stewart*

Northamptonshire Ironstone Railway Trust

Location: Hunsbury Hill Museum, Camp Hill, Hunsbury Hill Road, Northampton
Operating society/organisation: Northamptonshire Ironstone Railway Trust Ltd, c/o 5 Forest Road, Delapre, Northampton NN4 9NZ
Telephone: Northampton 62833
Car park: On site
Access by public transport: Terminus of Northampton Transport bus routes, 24, 25, 26 to Camp Hill from Northampton Greyfriars Bus station
On site facilities: Light refreshments, shop, small museum in main engine shed compound. Brake van rides available
Public opening: Sundays and bank holidays Easter-end September
Special notes: Disabled can be given rides in converted brake van

Industrial Locomotives

Name	*No*	*Builder*	*Type*	*Built*
Brill	—	M/Wardle (1795)	0-4-0ST	1912
—	—	Peckett (1871)	0-6-0ST	1934*
—	—	Peckett (2029)	0-6-0ST	1942*
Belvedere	—	Sentinel (9365)	0-4-0TG	1945
Musketeer	—	Sentinel (9369)	0-4-0TG	1945
—	—	Lister (14006)	0-4-0PM	1950†
—	—	R/Hornsby	0-4-0DM	1945
—	—	R/Hornsby	0-4-0DM	1950
—	—	Simplex (9711)	0-4-0DM	1945†
—	—	Simplex	0-4-0DM	1946†

*Metre gauge
†2ft gauge

National Tramway Museum

Location: Crich, near Matlock, Derbyshire DE4 5DP
Operating society/organisation: Tramway Museum Society
Telephone: 077 385 2565
Car park: Site, coach parking also available
Access by public transport: Trent bus services No 240. Nearest stations: Matlock (BR) or Alfreton & Mansfield Parkway (BR) then by bus; or Whatstandwell (BR) and steep uphill walk
On site facilities: Souvenir shop, cafe and picnic area. 1 mile electric tramway
Public opening: Saturdays, Sundays and Bank Holidays from April-October (10.30-17.00). Also Mondays-Thursdays Easter-end September 10.00-16.30
Special Notes: Crich houses the largest collection of preserved trams in Europe and has a 1 mile working tramway on which restored trams are operated. Annual 'Transport Extravaganzas' are held, when other vintage vehicles are present and special events are arranged. Part of tram line occupies route of narrow gauge mineral railway built by George Stephenson

Locomotives

Name	*No*	*Builder*	*Type*	*Built*
—	—	B/Peacock (2464)	0-4-0VB tram loco	1885
—	—	E/Electric	4wE	1927
Rupert	—	R/Hornsby (223741)	4wDM	1944
GMJ	—	R/Hornsby (326058)	4wDM	1952
—	—	R/Hornsby (373363)	4wDM	1954

Also some 40 trams including examples from Czechoslovakia, Portugal, USA and South Africa, about half of which have been restored to working order

Newcastle Corporation No 102 at Crich.
S. Keightley

Rutland Railway Museum

Location: Cottesmore Iron Ore Mines Siding, Ashwell Road, Cottesmore, near Oakham, Leicestershire — museum situated mid-way between villages of Cottesmore and Ashwell, approximately 4 miles north of Oakham).
Operating society/organisation: Rutland Railway Museum, Cottesmore Iron Ore Mines Siding, Ashwell Road, Cottesmore, Nr Oakham, Leicestershire
Telephone: (Information) Stamford 62384, Leicester 67637 or South Rauceby 267
Car park: On site
Access by public transport: Nearest BR station, Oakham. Blands bus service, Leicester-Oakham-Cottesmore. Bartons buses, Nottingham-Melton Mowbray-Oakham-Ashwell, Corby/Peterborough-Oakham-Ashwell (services 117 and 125).
On site facilities: Light refreshments, toilets, shop, picnic sites, approx $\frac{3}{4}$ mile length demonstration line with lineside walk and viewing areas
Public Opening: Open every weekend or by arrangement. Regular steam days: 22/23 April (Easter); 6/7 May (May Day Bank Holiday); 27/28 May (Spring Bank Holiday); 1 July; 11/12 August 'Summer Steam Weekend' (plus extra attractions); 26/27 August (Summer Bank Holiday); 30 September. 11.00-17.00pm
Facilities for disabled: Site relatively flat. Members willing to assist.
Special notes: The museum houses an extensive collecton of industrial locomotives and rolling stock typifying past activity in local ironstone quarries, nationwide mines and factories. A demonstration line approximately $\frac{3}{4}$-mile long has been relaid on the former MR Cottesmore mineral branch originally built to tap local ironstone quarries, on which restored locomotives and stock are run. Among the latter is the only surviving Wisbech & Upwell Tramway Coach

Industrial Locomotives

Name	*No*	*Builder*	*Type*	*Built*
Uppingham	—	Peckett (1257)	0-4-0ST	1912
—	2	Barclay (1931)	0-4-0ST	1927
Dora	—	Avonside (1973)	0-4-0ST	1927
Elizabeth	—	Peckett (1759)	0-4-0ST	1928
Singapore	Yard No 440	H/Leslie (3865)	0-4-0ST	1936
Sir Thomas Royden	—	Barclay (2088)	0-4-0ST	1940
—	—	Barclay (352)	0-4-0DM	1941
S and L No 24	—	Hunslet (2411)	0-6-0ST	1941
Salmon	8410/39	Barclay (2139)	0-6-0ST	1942
Coal Products No 6	—	Hunslet (2868)	0-6-0ST	1943
		(Rebuilt Hunslet 3883 1963)		
—	8	Peckett (2110)	0-4-0ST	1950
—	—	R/Hornsby (306092)	4wDM	1950
—	—	R/Hornsby (305302)	4wDM	1951
	DB965072	Wickham (7587)	2w-2PMR	1957
Phoenix	—	Hibberd (3887)	4wDM	1958
Janus	28	YEC (2791)	0-6-0DE	1962
Colsterworth	1382	YEC (2872)	0-6-0DE	1962
—	20-90-01	Barclay (499)	0-4-0DH	1965
—	20-90-02	R/Hornsby (504565)	0-4-0DH	1965

Stock
Over 50 items

Singapore giving brakevan rides during a museum open day. *J. Wade*

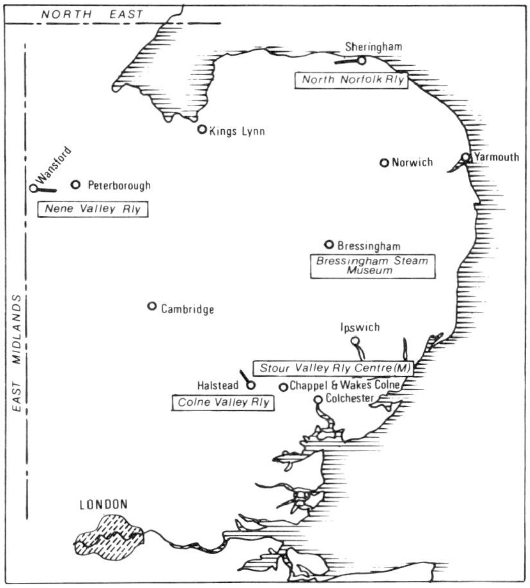

North Norfolk Railway

Headquarters: North Norfolk Railway, Sheringham station, Sheringham Norfolk, NR26 8RA
Telephone: Sheringham 822045
Main station: Sheringham
Other public stations: Weybourne
Car parks: Sheringham (old goods yard), Weybourne
Access by public transport: Sheringham BR station (200 yards)
Refreshment facilities: Sheringham, Weybourne
Souvenir shops: Sheringham, Weybourne
Museum: Sheringham
Depot: Weybourne
Passenger trains: Steeply graded, Sheringham-Weybourne (3 miles)
Period of public operation: Saturdays July-September. Sundays April-October. Tuesdays, Wednesdays and Thursdays July-September
Special Notes: Not all the stock is located on the line, but is in store at various sites in East Anglia
Feature article references: TI No 45 P4

Stock
2 WMB ex-BR diesel railbuses
6 ex-BR coaches
2 ex-SR 'Brighton Belle' Pullman cars
7 ex-LNER coaches
Small number of wagons

Locomotives

Name	*No*	*Origin*	*Class*	*Type*	*Built*
—	7564	GER	J15	0-6-0	1912
—	61572	LNER	B12	4-6-0	1928

Industrial locomotives

Name	*No*	*Builder*	*Type*	*Built*
Pony	—	H/Leslie (2918)	0-4-0ST	1912
Ring Haw	—	Hunslet (1982)	0-6-0ST	1940
Harlaxton	—	Barclay (2107)	0-6-0T	1941
Birchenwood	4	Bagnall (2680)	0-6-0ST	1944
John D Hamer	5	Peckett (1970)	0-6-0ST	1939
—	12	RSH (7845)	0-6-0T	1955
Colwyn	45	Kitson (5470)	0-6-0ST	1933
Dr Harry	—	Fowler (410001)	4wDM	1945
—	10	E/Electric C8431	0-4-0DH	1963
—	4	Fowler	4wDM	1953
Wissington	—	H/Clarke (1700)	0-6-0ST	1938
—	—	Bagnall	0-6-0F	—

Owners
7564 (the Midland and Great Northern Railway Society)
61572 (the Midland and Great Northern Railway Society)

No 7564 passes No 61572 as it arrives at Weybourne on 29 August 1982. *B. Fisher*

Nene Valley Railway

Headquarters: Nene Valley Railway, Wansford station, Old North Road, Stibbington, Wansford, near Peterborough, Cambs
Telephone: Stamford 782854
Main station: Wansford
Other public stations: Orton Mere, Ferry Meadows.
Car park: Wansford
Access by public transport: Buses from Peterborough to Orton Mere and Ferry Meadows. Special DMU service Peterborough-Orton Mere (certain dates only)
Refreshment facilities: Wansford
Souvenir shops: Wansford, Orton Mere, Ferry Meadows
Museum: Wansford
Depot: Wansford
Passenger trains: Wansford-Orton Mere
Length of line: 5 miles
Period of public operation: Weekends April-September and Bank Holidays, Wednesdays and Thursdays June, July and August
Facilities for disabled: Ramp access to all stations and shops. Toilets adjacent to Wansford station souvenir shop. Disabled persons and helpers are eligible for concessionary fares. Passengers can be assisted on and off trains
Feature article references: RW December 1983 p646

Locomotives

Name	*No*	*Origin*	*Class*	*Type*	*Built*
—	656	DSR	F	0-6-0T	1949
Danish Seaways	740	DSR	S	2-6-4T	1927
—	1697	SJ	B	4-6-0	1943
—	1178	SJ	S	2-6-2T	1914
—	1928	SJ	S1	2-6-4T	1953
—	3.628	SNCF	230D	4-6-0	1911
92 Squadron	34081	SR	BB	4-6-2	1948
Britannia	70000	BR	7MT	4-6-2	1951
City of Peterborough	73050	BR	5MT	4-6-0	1954
Royal Scots Grey	D9000	BR	55	Co-Co	1961
Gordon Highlander	55.016	BR	55	Co-Co	1961
—	064-305-6	DB	64	2-6-2T	1936
—	80.014	DB	80	0-6-0T	1927

Industrial locomotives

Name	*No*	*Builder*	*Type*	*Built*
—	—	Avonside (1945)	0-6-0ST	1926
—	90432	Barclay (2248)	0-4-0ST	1948
Derek Crouch	—	H/Clarke (1539)	0-6-0ST	1924
Thomas	—	H/Clarke (1800)	0-6-0T	1947
Jacks Green	—	Hunslet (1953)	0-6-0ST	1939
—	75006	Hunslet (2855)	0-6-0ST	1943
—	—	Peckett (2000)	0-6-0ST	1942

Stock
BR Mk 1 coaches
Ex-SR 4-COR electric unit and two other ex-EMU vehicles
Various European coaches

Owners
34081 (the Battle of Britain Locomotive Preservation Society)
73050 (Peterborough City Council)
3.628 (Science Museum)
Ex-SR electric stock (the Southern Electric Group)
70000 (the Britannia Locomotive Society)
D9000 and 55.016 (the D9000 Preservation Group)

Swedish 2-6-2T No 1178 departs from Orton Mere, 30 April 1983. *J. Wade*

Colne Valley Railway

Location: Castle Hedingham station, Yeldham Road, Castle Hedingham, Halstead, Essex CO9 3DZ

Locomotives

Name	*No*	*Origin*	*Class*	*Type*	*Built*
—	1 (D2041)	BR	03	0-6-0DM	1959

Operating society/organisation: Colne Valley Railway Preservation Society
Telephone: Hedingham 61174
Car park: At the site (access from A604 road) between Castle Hedingham and Gt Yeldham
Access by public transport: Eastern National bus services No 88 Colchester-Halstead, 89 Halstead-Hedingham and Hedingham & District Nos 4 Braintree-Hedingham, 5 Sudbury-Hedingham. Nearest BR station — Braintree
On site facilities: Depot, museum, souvenir shop and refreshments, $3\frac{1}{2}$ acre wooded picnic area, toilets
Public opening: Daily for static displays except Christmas, New Year and January. Locomotives in steam on 1st and 3rd Sunday of the month between Easter and October inclusive, also every bank holiday and preceeding Sunday except Christmas and New Year. Schools week in June
Length of line: $\frac{3}{4}$ mile
Facilities for disabled: To look and ride only
Special notes: The railway has been completely rebuilt on part of the original Colne Valley line track-bed. The railway offers much of educational value specialising in school party visits by appointment at any time of the year.

Industrial locomotives

Name	No	Builder	Type	Built
Victory	—	Barclay (2199)	0-4-0ST	1945
Castle Hedingham	—	Hunslet (3790)	0-6-0ST	1952
—	72	Vulcan (5309)	0-6-0ST	1945
—	40	RSH (7765)	0-6-0T	1954
Barrington	—	Avonside (1875)	0-4-0ST	1921
—	1	H/Leslie (3715)	0-4-0ST	1928
—	—	R/Hornsby	0-4-0DM	1943
—	—	Hibbard (3147)	0-4-0DM	1947

Stock
7 ex-BR Mk1 coaches and sundry items of freight stock.
1 ex-Norwegian State Railway Class B 65 No 18803 (built 1926) Balcony Open Second (teak)
1 ex-'Brighton Belle' Pullman car, *Gwen*
Steam crane DRG 80103

***Castle Hedingham* carrying her War Department number.** *J. D. Mann*

Stour Valley Railway Centre

Location: Chappel & Wakes Colne station, near Colchester
Operating society/organisation: Stour Valley Railway Preservation Society, Chappel & Wakes Colne station, Essex
Car park: Chappel
Access by public transport: Chappel & Wakes Colne BR station
On site facilities: Light refreshments, and bookshop
Public opening: Every weekend 11.00-18.00
Special notes: Special steam days are held first Sunday of month March-October inclusive, plus Bank Holidays. Collection of pre-1900 six and four-wheel passenger stock being restored to form a vintage train

Locomotives

Name	No	Origin	Class	Type	Built
—	999	GER	N7	0-6-2T	1924
—	80151	BR	4MT	2-6-4T	1956

Industrial locomotives

Name	No	Builder	Type	Built
Jubilee	—	Bagnall (2541)	0-4-0ST	1936
—	1074	Barclay (1047)	0-4-0ST	1905
Belvoir	—	Barclay (2305)	0-6-0ST	1954
Gunby	68067	Hunslet (2413)	0-6-0ST	1941
—	2	M/Vick	0-4-0E	1912
—	1438	Peckett (1438)	0-4-0ST	1916
—	2039	Peckett (2039)	0-4-0ST	1943
—	54	RSH (7013)	0-6-0ST	1941
Jupiter	—	RSH (7671)	0-6-0T	1950
—	AMW144	Barclay (333)	0-4-0DM	1938
—	23	Fowler (4220039)	0-4-0DH	1965
—	2029	Simplex	0-4-0PM	1920

Stock
1 ex-LNER coach
6 ex-BR Mk1 coaches
1 ex-BR sleeping coach
1 ex-BR prototype Bar Car
1 ex-LNER Buffet car
1 GER 6-wheel full brake
1 GER 6-wheel family saloon
1 GER 4-wheel coach
2 MSL 6-wheel coaches
4 GER coach bodies
Small number of wagons
Grafton 4ton steam crane

Lincolnshire Coast Light Railway

Location: St Anthony's Bank, Humberston, Grimsby, Humberside DN36 4EP
Operating society/organisation: Lincolnshire Coast Light Railway Co Ltd, Laxfield, Fotherby, Louth, Lincs LN11 0UH
Car park: Adjacent to North Sea Lane station
Access by public transport: Grimsby-Cleethorpes Transport from Grimsby Town and Cleethorpes BR station. Route 17 stops adjacent
On site facilities: Refreshments and sales kiosk
Period of public operation: Details from Grimsby 42826
Facilities for disabled: Ramps for wheelchairs
Feature article references: RW July 1983 p355

Industrial locomotives

Name	*No*	*Builder*	*Type*	*Built*
Paul	1	M/Rail (3995)	4wDM	1927
Jurassic	2	Peckett (1008)	0-6-0ST	1903
Elin	3	Hunslet (705)	0-4-0ST	1899
Wilton	4	M/Rail (7481)	4wDM	1940
—	5	M/Rail (8622)	4wDM	1941
—	6	M/Rail (8874)	4wDM	1944
Nocton	7	M/Rail (1935)	4wDM	1920

Stock
5 coaches
Small quantity of wagons

Bressingham Steam Museum

Location: Two miles west of Diss on the A1066
Operating society/organisation: Bressingham Steam Preservation Co Ltd, Bressingham Hall, Diss, Norfolk R22 2AB
Telephone: Bressingham 386
Car park: Steam Centre (free)
Access by public transport: Diss BR station (3 miles). Bus meets 10.30 train from Liverpool Street
On site facilities: $9\frac{1}{2}$/15/24in and standard gauge lines, totalling nearly 5 miles. Museum, steam roundabout, souvenir shop and cafeteria, extensive gardens
Public opening: Thursdays early June-6 September 13.30-17.30. Sundays and Bank Holidays from early May-late September, 13.30-18.00. Wednesdays during August 13.30-17.30
Facilities for disabled: Toilets
Special notes: Reduced rates for coach parties. Maximum admission £1 adults

Locomotives

Name	*No*	*Origin*	*Class*	*Type*	*Built*
Martello	62	LBSCR	A1X	0-6-0T	1875
Thundersley	80	LTSR	3P	4-4-2T	1909
Granville	102	LSWR	B4	0-4-0T	1893
—	1217E	GER	J17	0-6-0	1905
—	2500	LMS	4MT	2-6-4T	1934
Royal Scot	6100	LMS	7P	4-6-0	1927
Duchess of Sutherland	6233	LMS	8P	4-6-2	1938
Oliver Cromwell	70013	BR	7MT	4-6-2	1951
Peer Gynt	5865	NSB	52	2-10-0	1944
Tom Paine	141R73	SNCF	141R	2-8-2	1945
King Haakon VII	377	NSB	—	2-6-0	1919

Industrial locomotives

Name	*No*	*Builder*	*Type*	*Built*
Beckton	1	Neilson (4444)	0-4-0WT	1892
Beckton	25	Neilson (5087)	0-4-0ST	1896
William Francis	6841	B/Peacock	0-4-4-0	1937
Millfield	—	RSH (7070)	0-4-0CT	1942
Bluebottle	—	Barclay	0-4-0F	

Stanier 2-6-4T No 2500 in action at Bressingham, June 1983. *B. Avery*

Owners
62, 102, 6100, 6233 (Butlins)
80, 1217E, 2500, 70013 (on loan from the National Railway Museum)

Narrow gauge locomotives

Gwynedd	—	Hunslet (316)	0-4-0ST	1883
George Sholto	—	Hunslet (994)	0-4-0ST	1909
Bronllwyd	—	H/Clarke (1643)	0-6-0WT	1930
Eigiau	—	O&K (5668)	0-4-0WT	1912
—	—	R&H (437367)	4wDM	1959
—	—	M/Rail (22210)	4wDM	1964
—	—	M/Rail (22253)	4wDM	1965

15in gauge locomotives

Rosenkavalier	—	Krupp (1662)	4-6-2	1937
Mannertreu	—	Krupp (1663)	4-6-2	1937
Flying Scotsman	4472	W. Stewart (4472)	4-6-2	1976

9½in gauge locomotive

Princess	—	Motor Gear & Engine Co	4-6-2	1947

NORTH-WEST

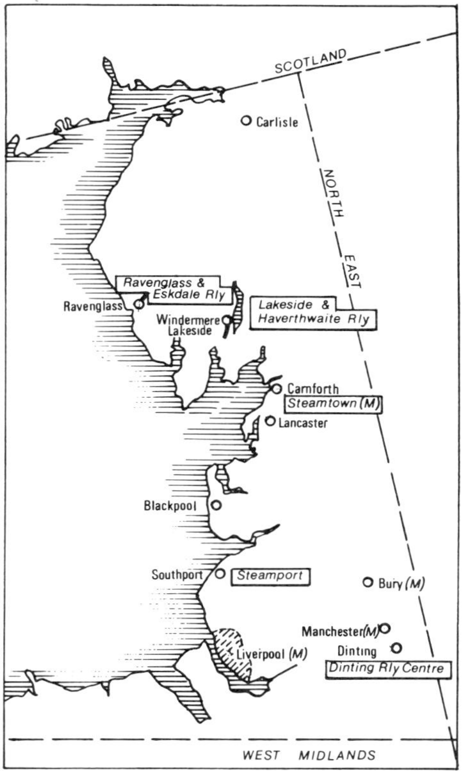

No 2085 receives attention while awaiting to depart from Haverthwaite in September 1982. *T. Grimshaw*

Lakeside and Haverthwaite Railway

Headquarters: Haverthwaite station, near Ulverston, Cumbria LA12 8AL
Telephone: Newby Bridge 31594
Main station: Haverthwaite
Other public stations: Intermediate station at Newby Bridge. Terminus at Lakeside

Locomotives

Name	*No*	*Origin*	*Class*	*Type*	*Built*
—	2073	LMS	4MT	2-6-4T	1950
—	2085	LMS	4MT	2-6-4T	1951
—	8(D2117)	BR	03	0-6-0DM	1959
—	17(AD601)	LMS	—	0-6-0DE	1945
—	03.072	BR	03	0-6-0DM	1959

Car parks: Haverthwaite, Lakeside
Access by public transport: Sealink ships on Lake Windermere call at Lakeside. Ribble bus to Haverthwaite
Refreshment facilities: Haverthwaite
Souvenir shop: Haverthwaite
Depot: All rolling stock at Haverthwaite
Passenger trains: Steam-hauled Haverthwaite-Lakeside ($3\frac{1}{2}$miles)
Period of public operation: Easter then daily from early-May to end of September. Sundays only in October.
Special notes: Combined railway/lake steamer tickets available, from the station at Haverthwaite and Sealink piers at Bowness and Ambleside

Stock
12 ex-BR Mk1 coaches
1 ex-LNER BG
1 ex-BR Mk1 miniature buffet coach
Small selection of freight vehicles

Industrial locomotives

Name	*No*	*Builder*	*Type*	*Built*
Caliban	1	Peckett (1925)	0-4-0ST	1937
Fluff	16	Hunslet/Fowler	0-4-0DM	1937
—	5	H/Clarke (1631)	0-6-0ST	1929
Renishaw Ironworks No 6	6	H/Clarke (1366)	0-6-0ST	1919
Rachel	9	M/Rail	4w tram	1924
Repulse	11	Hunslet (3698)	0-6-0ST	1950
Princess	14	Bagnall (2682)	0-6-0ST	1942
Askam Hall	15	Avonside/H/Leslie	0-4-0ST	1935
Alexandra	12	Barclay (929)	0-4-0ST	1902
David	13	Barclay 2333)	0-4-0ST	1953
Cumbria	10	Hunslet (3794)	0-6-0ST	1953
Miranda	2	Peckett	0-4-0ST	1948
—	7	Fowler (22919)	0-4-0DM	1940
—	18	Fowler	0-4-0DM	1948
—	20	Jones crane	0-4-0DM	1952
—	21	Barclay (1550)	0-6-0F	1917
—	22	Fowler	0-4-0DM	1967
—	23	Fowler	0-4-0DM	1967

Bury Transport Museum

Location: Bury Transport Museum, Castlecroft Road, Bury, Lancashire BL9 0LN
Operating society/organisation: East Lancashire Railway Preservation Society
Telephone: 061 764 7790
Car park: Castlecroft Road and Bolton Street
Access by public transport: BR to Bury (not Sunday). Greater Manchester Transport, Rossendale Transport and Ribble Motor Services to Bury
On site facilities: Refreshments, usually served in buffet coach, available on Sundays, and also on steam days, souvenir shop
Public opening: Saturdays and Sundays throughout the year and bank holiday Mondays March to September. Steam-hauled brake van rides on last Sunday of month and on Sunday and Monday at Bank Holiday Weekends between March and September
Special Notes: Model railway operating on steam days

Locomotives

Name	*No*	*Origin*	*Class*	*Type*	*Built*
Taw Valley	34027	SR	WC	4-6-2	1946
—	D2587	BR	05	0-6-0DM	1959
—	D2595	BR	05	0-6-0DM	1959
—	D2767	BR	—	0-4-0DM	1960
—	D5054	BR	24	Bo-Bo	1960
Onslaught	D832	BR	42	B-B	1961
Western Prince	D1041	BR	52	C-C	1962
—	D7076	BR	35	B-B	1963

Industrial locomotives

Name	*No*	*Builder*	*Type*	*Built*
Gothenburg	32	H/Clarke (680)	0-6-0T	1903
Phoenix	70	H/Clarke (1464)	0-6-0T	1921
Annie	945	Barclay (945)	0-4-0ST	1904
—	1	Barclay (1927)	0-4-0ST	1927
—	62	RSH (7673)	0-6-0ST	1950
MEA No 1	1	RSH (7683)	0-6-0T	1951

2 4-wheel diesel mechanical locomotives

Stock
9 BR coaches
1 L&YR coach
Cravens 50ton steam crane No RS1013/50 (1930) and NER 5ton Hand crane No DB915390 (1880) plus a small number of other goods vehicles

'Warship' class No D832 *Onslaught*.
R. Anthony

Dinting Railway Centre

Location: Dinting Railway Centre Ltd, Dinting, Glossop, Derbyshire
Operating society/organisation: Bahamas Locomotive Society
Telephone: Glossop 5596
Car park: Free parking on site
Access by public transport: BR services to Dinting station and buses Nos 215, 236, 237 and 394
On site facilities: Refreshments and souvenir shop. Picnic area. Miniature steam railway (Bank Holiday and certain Sundays)
Public opening: Daily except Christmas and Boxing Day. Locomotives in steam and brakevan rides available Sundays and Bank Holidays from March-October. Also New Year's day
Special notes: Dinting is a centre for steam-hauled main line railtours

Stock
Sundry freight vehicles

Locomotives

Name	*No*	*Origin*	*Class*	*Type*	*Built*
Bahamas	5596	LMS	'Jubilee'	4-6-0	1935
Scots Guardsman	6115	LMS	'Royal Scot'	4-6-0	1927
—	102	GCR	04	2-8-0	1911
—	1054	LNWR	—	0-6-2T	1888
Blue Peter	532	LNER	A2/3	4-6-2	1948
Bittern	19	LNER	A4	4-6-2	1937

Industrial locomotives

Name	*No*	*Builder*	*Type*	*Built*
Southwick	—	RSH (7069)	0-4-0CT	1942
Warrington	150	RSH (7136)	0-6-0ST	1944
Nunlow	—	H/Clarke (1704)	0-6-0T	1938
—	1883	Avonside (1883)	0-6-0ST	1923
Tiny	—	Barclay (2258)	0-4-0ST	1949
—	—	B/Peacock (2734)	0-4-0VB tram	1886
—	RS8	Avonside/RR (1913)	0-4-0DH	1923
Jacob	—	McEwan Pratt (680)	Petrol loco	1916

Owners
1054 (the National Trust)
102 (on loan from the National Railway Museum)

Steamport, Southport

Location: Five minutes from BR station, via London Street. Behind car park

Locomotives

Name	*No*	*Origin*	*Class*	*Type*	*Built*
—	5193	GWR	5101	2-6-2T	1934
—	76079	BR	4MT	2-6-0	1957
Cecil Raikes	5	Mersey Railway	—	0-6-4T	1886
—	24.081	BR	24	Bo-Bo	1958
Western Lady	D1048	BR	52	C-C	1962

Locomotive line up at Southport, left to right, *North Western Gas Board*, *Waleswood* and *Efficient*. *D. Rawlinson*

Operating society/organisation: Steamport Southport Ltd, Derby Road, Southport PR9 0TY
Telephone: Southport 30693
Car park: Derby Road
Access by public transport: BR station, Merseyrail from Liverpool
On site facilities: Souvenir shop/cafe at weekends. Steam hauled rides in LMS brake vans May-end September, plus special events
Length of line: 600yd
Public opening: October-April 14.00-17.00 Weekends. May-September 11.00-17.00 Weekends. Weekdays June-mid September 13.00-17.00. Daily July-August 11.00-17.00
Facilities for disabled: Access to all parts of museum. No toilets. No advanced notice required
Feature article reference: RW June 1982 p298

Industrial locomotives

Name	*No*	*Builder*	*Type*	*Built*
—	5	Peckett (2153)	0-6-0ST	1954
North Western Gas Board	—	Peckett (1999)	0-4-0ST	1941
Waleswood	—	H/Clarke (750)	0-4-0ST	1906
Kinsley	—	Hunslet (1954)	0-6-0ST	1939
Glasshaughton	4	Hunslet (3855)	0-6-0ST	1954
Persil	—	Fowler (4160001)	0-4-0DM	1952
*Lucy**	—	Avonside (1568)	0-6-0ST	1909
*Efficient**	—	Barclay (1598)	0-4-0ST	1918
St Monans	—	Sentinel (9373)	4wVBT	1947
Hornet	—	Peckett (1935)	0-4-0ST	1937
Whitehead	—	Peckett (1163)	0-4-0ST	1908
—	—	Peckett (1990)	0-4-0ST	1941
—	—	Greenwood & Batley (2000)	0-4-0BE	1958
Sefton	—	T/Hill (123V)	0-4-0DH	1963
—	DH1	YEC (2677)	0-4-0DM	1960
—	DH2	YEC (2820)	0-4-0DM	1960

Stock
Small selection of rolling stock including Class 502 emu, M28361M and M29896M on loan from NRM

Owner
Cecil Raikes (on loan from National Railway Museum/Liverpool Museum)
Stock* (Liverpool Locomotive Preservation Group)

Steamtown, Carnforth

Location: Steamtown Railway Museum Ltd, Warton Road, Carnforth, Lancashire LA5 9HX
Operating society/organisation: Steamtown Railway Musuem Ltd
Telephone: Carnforth 732100/734220
Car park: Free car park on site
Access by public transport: BR services to Carnforth station. Bus services to Carnforth by Ribble and Lancaster City Transport
On site facilities: Model railway, signalbox, collectors' corner, shop, cafe, 15in gauge railway
Public opening: Daily 09.00-17.00 except Christmas Day. Locomotives in steam on Bank Holidays, Sundays from Easter-October, and daily during July-August
Special notes: Formerly BR Carnforth motive power depot. Carnforth is a centre for 'Steam on BR' steam-hauled railtours over BR main lines. Scheduled steam hauled excursions during summer season, operate from Carnforth with through connections from main centres
Feature article references: RW January 1982; RW October 1982 p516 (locomotive 4498); RW July 1983 p359 (locomotive 4498)

Locomotives

Name	*No*	*Origin*	*Class*	*Type*	*Built*
Flying Scotsman	4472	LNER	A3	4-6-2	1923
Sir Nigel Gresley	4498	LNER	A4	4-6-2	1937
Canadian Pacific	35005	SR	MN	4-6-2	1941
Lord Nelson	850	SR	LN	4-6-0	1926
—	5643	GWR	5600	0-6-2T	1925
—	9629	GWR	9600	0-6-0PT	1945
Sovereign	44871	LMS	5MT	4-6-0	1945
—	44932	LMS	5MT	4-6-0	1945
—	5407	LMS	5MT	4-6-0	1937
—	6441	LMS	2MT	2-6-0	1950
—	1300	L&Y	—	0-6-0	1896
—	D2381	BR	03	0-6-0	1960
La France	231K22	SNCF	231K	4-6-2	1914
—	01.1104	DB	01	4-6-2	1940

As well as having British Pacifics on site Steamtown also houses two Continental examples, this is SNCF 231K22 of 1914.

Stock

10 pre-Grouping saloon coaches
1 LNER buffet car
4 BR Mk 1 coaches
Small selection of freight vehicles
2 steam cranes

Owners

1300 (the Fairclough Corporation)
4498 (the A4 Locomotive Society)
850 (on loan from the National Railway Museum)

Industrial locomotives

Name	No	Builder	Type	Built
Sirapite	6158	A/Porter	0-4-0	1906
Pitsford	—	Avonside (1917)	0-6-0ST	1923
Tom Rolt	7049	Hunslet (2697)	0-6-0DM	1944
John Howe	5	Barclay (1147)	0-4-0ST	1908
Jane Darbyshire	2	Barclay (1969)	0-4-0ST	1929
Coronation	3	Barclay (2134)	0-4-0ST	1942
Cooke & Nuttal	1	Barclay (2320)	0-4-0ST	1947
British Gypsum	4	Barclay (2343	0-4-0ST	1953
Glenfield	1	Barclay (880)	0-4-0CT	1902
May	—	Peckett (1370)	0-4-0ST	1915
Trimpell	—	Bagnall (3019)	0-6-0F	1953
Cranford No 2	—	Bagnall (2668)	0-6-0ST	1942
Firefly	1	Hudswell (1864)	0-6-0T	1942
Great Central	39	RSH(6947)	0-6-0T	1938
—	7	S/Stewart (1435)	0-6-0ST	1863
Lindsay	—	Wigan Coal & Iron Co	0-6-0ST	1887
Flying Flea	D3	R/Hornsby	0-4-0DM	1951
Gasbag	7	Sentinel (8024)	4wVBTG	1929
Esso	—	General Electric (30483)	Co-Co	1942

Ravenglass and Eskdale Railway

Headquarters: Ravenglass and Eskdale Railway, Ravenglass station, Cumbria
Telephone: 06577 226
Main station: Ravenglass
Other public stations: Muncaster, Irton Road, The Green, Eskdale (Dalegarth)
Car parks: Ravenglass, Dalegarth
Access by public transport: BR services to Ravenglass. CMS buses between Whitehaven and Millom call at Ravenglass
Refreshment facilities: Ravenglass, Dalegarth
Souvenir shops: Ravenglass, Dalegarth
Museum: Ravenglass
Passenger trains: Steam or diesel-hauled (15in) narrow gauge trains Ravenglass-Dalegarth (7 miles)
Period of public operation: Daily from late March-late October. Limited winter service November-March
Facilities for disabled: Special coaches for wheel-chair passengers. Advanced notice preferred. Wheelchair access to toilets at Ravenglass; Museum; shop and cafe at Eskdale (Dalegarth)
Special notes: At Ravenglass the R&ER has two camping coaches and the company also operates the 'Ratty Arms' public house formed by conversion of the former BR station buildings. 'Cumbrian Coast Express' steam-operated tours call at Ravenglass leaving sufficient time for trip on R&ER

Locomotives

Name	No	Builder	Type	Built
River Mite	—	Clarkson (4669)	2-8-2	1966
Northern Rock	—	R&ER	2-6-2	1975
River Irt	—	Heywood	0-8-2	1894
River Esk	—	Davey Paxman (21104)	2-8-2	1923
Shelagh of Eskdale	—	R&ER/Severn-Lamb	4-6-4DH	1968
Quarryman	—	Muir-Hill	0-4-0P/Paraffin	1925
Pretender	—	Muir Hill	0-4-2DM	1929
Silver Jubilee	—	R&ER	dmu	1977
Bonny Dundee	—	K/Stuart	0-4-2	1900
Lady Wakefield	—	R&ER	Bo-Bo	1980
Synolda	—	Bassett-Lowke	4-4-2	1912
—	—	Greenbat	0-4-0B	1957

A diesel-hauled train leaving Ravenglass in April 1983. *M. H. C. Baker*

Liverpool Museum

Location: William Brown Street, Liverpool
Operating society/organisation: Merseyside County Museums, William Brown Street, Liverpool L3 8EN
Telephone: 051-207 0001
Car parks: Public car parks nearby
Access by public transport: Adjacent Lime Street stations (BR and Merseyrail). Numerous bus routes both MPTE and Ribble
On site facilities: Cafe (closed at weekends) shop
Public opening: 10.00-17.00 Monday-Saturday, 14.00-17.00 Sunday
Special notes: Transport gallery within large general museum. Facilities for disabled visitors

Locomotive

Name	*No*	*Origin*	*Class*	*Type*	*Built*
Lion	57	L&MR	—	0-4-2	1838

Industrial Locomotive

Name	*No*	*Builder*	*Type*	*Built*
—	1	Avonside (1465)	0-6-0ST	1904

Stock
LOR electric coach of 1893
L&MR replica coaches

Flashback to 1980 with *Lion* waiting to steam into Liverpool Road station. Seen at Eccles on 14 September. *A. Oldfield*

Greater Manchester Museum of Science and Industry

Location: Liverpool Road Station, Manchester (off Deansgate near Granada and Air and Space Museum)
Operating society/organisation: Greater Manchester Museum of Science and Industry, Liverpool Road Station, Liverpool Road, Castlefield, Manchester M3 4JP
Car parks: On site, plus parking in the area
Access by public transport: Manchester Victoria, Picadilly and Oxford Road BR stations. GMT buses 15, 70, 166
On site facilities: Shop, displays, working scientific, industrial and railway exhibits, train rides, guided tours of oldest passenger station, cafe
Public opening: Daily including Saturdays and Sundays 10.30-17.00. Entrance in Lower Byron Street. No charge
Special notes: Not suitable for severely disabled

Locomotives

Name	*No*	*Builder*	*Type*	*Built*
—	44806	LMS (5MT)	4-6-0	1944
—	3157*	V/Foundry	4-4-0	1911
Pender	3†	B/Peacock (1255)	2-4-0T	1873
—	—	A/Barclay (1964)	0-4-0ST	1929
Agecroft No 3	—	RSH (7681)	0-4-0ST	1951
—	—	E/Electric (1378)	4wBE	1944
—	—	H/Leslie (3682)	Bo-Bo	1927
—	—	Fowler	0-6-0	—

*Ex-Pakistan Railways, 5ft 6in gauge
†Ex-IoMR, 3ft gauge, sectioned

NORTH-EAST

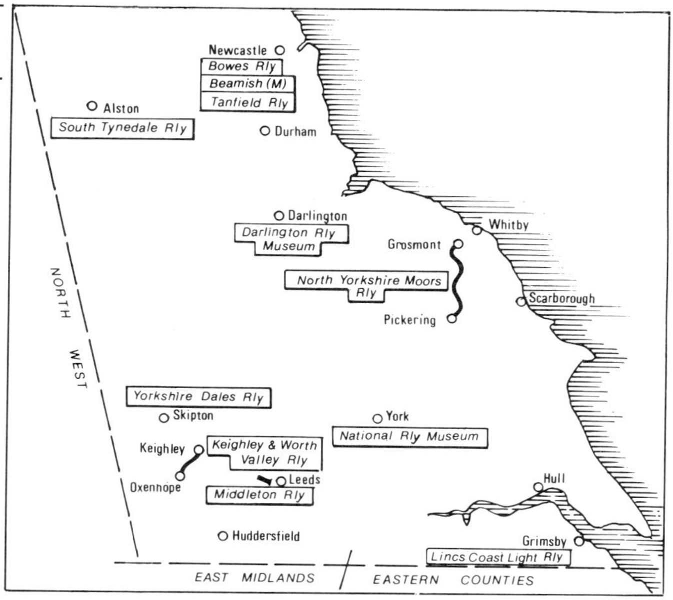

Keighley and Worth Valley Railway

Headquarters: Haworth station, Keighley, West Yorkshire, BD22 8NJ
Telephone: Haworth 43629 (talking timetable) Haworth 45214 (other calls)
Main stations: Haworth, Oxenhope, Keighley
Other public stations: Ingrow, Damens, Oakworth
Car parks: Oxenhope, Haworth, Oakworth and Ingrow; also in Keighley and Haworth
Access by public transport: A large number of bus routes serve the area including National coach routes Nos 281/2/5/9, 291, 307/8, 318; from Bradford Interchange, MetroBus 665/666/667/668 to Keighley. From Leeds, MetroBus 760 to Keighley. From Halifax, MetroBus 500 via Hebden Bridge to Oxenhope, MetroBus 502 via Denholme to Ingrow, Tel Halifax 65985 for timings. From Todmorden, MetroBus 501 via Hebden Bridge to Oxenhope. (Operates every Saturday throughout the year and Mon-Fri, mid-July to end August). Tel Halifax 65985 for timings. From Lancashire Coast/Preston/Burnley/Nelson, Ribble service to Burnley, then Burnley and Pendle/West Yorks Road Car Service 25 to Keighley bus station (Mon-Sat) or Keighley Rail Station (Sunday only). Use Trans-Lancs through ticket, buy at Ribble, Burnley and Pendle Bus Stations.
Refreshment facilities: Buffets at Keighley, Haworth and Oxenhope (normally open when steam trains are operating); buffet car on some trains
Souvenir shops: Haworth, Oxenhope, Keighley

Locomotives

Name	*No*	*Origin*	*Class*	*Type*	*Built*
—	43924	MR	4F	0-6-0	1920
—	42765	LMS	5PF	2-6-0	1927
—	41241	LMS	2MT	2-6-2T	1949
—	45212	LMS	5MT	4-6-0	1935
—	8431	LMS	8F	2-8-0	1944
—	47279	LMS	3F	0-6-0T	1925
City of Wells	34092	SR	WC	4-6-2	1949
—	80002	BR	4MT	2-6-4T	1952
—	75078	BR	4MT	4-6-0	1956
—	78022	BR	2MT	2-6-0	1953
—	72	SR	USA	0-6-0T	1943
—	L89 (5775)	GWR	5700	0-6-0PT	1929
—	4612	GWR	5700	0-6-0PT	1933
—	52044	L&Y	2F	0-6-0	1887
—	19	L&Y	Pug	0-4-0ST	1910
—	51218	L&Y	Pug	0-4-0ST	1901
—	752	L&Y	—	0-6-0ST	1881
—	52	TVR	02	0-6-2T	1899
—	5820	USA TC	S160	2-8-0	1945
—	1931	SJ	WD	2-8-0	1945
—	68077	LNER	J94	0-6-0ST	1947
—	D0266	BR	—	0-6-0DE	1956
—	D2511	BR	—	0-6-0DM	1961
—	D2519	BR	—	0-6-0DM	1961

Industrial locomotives

Name	*No*	*Builder*	*Type*	*Built*
Fred	—	RSH (7289)	0-6-0ST	1945
—	57	RSH (7668)	0-6-0ST	1950
—	63	RSH (7761)	0-6-0ST	1954
—	2226	Barclay (2226)	0-4-0ST	1946
Bellerophon	—	Haydock Foundry (C)	0-6-0WT	1874
Sir Berkeley	—	M/Wardle (1210)	0-6-0ST	1890
Lord Mayor	—	H/Clarke (402)	0-4-0ST	1893

Museums: Oxenhope (open when trains run); Haworth Yard open daily (except Christmas)
Depots: Oxenhope, Haworth, Oakworth, Ingrow
Passenger trains: Steam-hauled services from Oxenhope-Keighley (5 miles). Some off-peak and local shoppers' services worked by diesel railbus
Period of public operation: Winter (diesel) service November-March. Steam/diesel service weekends March-October. Daily during July/August. Spring Bank Holiday week and Christmas-New Year holiday week. Please note steam services Sundays Oxenhope-Haworth November; January and February. Winter steam December (Santa Sundays) Oakworth-Oxenhope
Facilities for disabled: Toilet on Haworth station forecourt. Wheelchairs accommodated in guard's compartments on trains. Please advise before visit to the Advanced Bookings Manager c/o Haworth station
Special notes: Accompanied children under 5 years of age free
Feature article reference: RW September 1983 p466; TI No 45 p16

Name	No	Builder	Type	Built
Hamburg	31	H/Clarke (697)	0-6-0T	1903
—	67	H/Clarke (1397)	0-6-0T	1919
Brussels	118	H/Clarke (1782)	0-6-0ST	1915
Austins No1	—	Peckett (5003)	0-4-0DM	1961
—	MDHB No 32	Hunslet (2699)	0-6-0DM	1944
—	ESC32	H/Clarke (D816)	0-4-0DM	1954
—	BSC34	H/Clarke (D990)	0-4-0DM	1954
—	BSC38	H/Clarke (D995)	0-4-0DM	1954

Stock
2 ex-BR German-built Waggon und Maschinenbau diesel railbuses
29 coaches including examples of pre-Grouping types, BR Mk1 stock and a Pullman car

Owners
19 (L&Y Saddletanks)
752 (L&Y Saddletanks)
51218 (L&Y Saddletanks)
43924 (the Midland 4F Preservation Society)
47279 (South Yorkshire 3F Fund)
75078 (the Standard 4 Preservation Society)
78022 (the Standard 4 Preservation Society)

Middleton Railway

Headquarters: Middleton Railway Trust Ltd
Telephone: (0532) 645 424
Main station: Tunstall Road platform off Moor Road
Car parks: Tunstall Road/Moor Road (free)
Access by public transport: Bus routes Nos 74 and 76 from Leeds City station
Refreshment facilities: Tunstall Road
Souvenir shop: Tunstall Road
Museum: Collection of locomotives, a loco shed is planned for 1984
Passenger trains: Steam hauled services over a $1\frac{1}{4}$ miles section of line
Period of public operation: Most weekends from Easter to end September and Bank Holidays. Trains depart at $\frac{1}{2}$-hourly intervals 14.00-16.30. Saturday trains may be diesel hauled
Facilities for disabled: Access very good. It is hoped to have disabled toilets available for 1984
Special notes: This is a preserved section of the country's oldest industrial railway, believed to date from 1758. Visitors ride in open goods wagons

Locomotives

Name	No	Origin	Class	Type	Built
—	1310	NER	Y7	0-4-0T	1891
—	54	LNER	Y1	0-4-0VB	1933
—	385	DSB	Hs	0-4-0WT	1893
—*	7051	LMS	—	0-6-0DM	1932

Industrial locomotives

Name	No	Builder	Type	Built
John Blenkinsop	2003	Peckett (2003)	0-4-0ST	1941
Henry de Lacy II	—	H/Clarke (1309)	0-4-0ST	1917
Windle	—	Borrows (53)	0-4-0WT	1909
Matthew Murray	—	Bagnall (2702)	0-4-0ST	1943
—	No 6	H/Leslie (3860)	0-4-0ST	1935
Carroll	—	H/Clarke (D631)	0-4-0DM	1946
Courage	—	Hunslet (1786)	4wD	1935
Mary	D577	H/Clarke (D577)	0-4-0DM	1932
—	3900002	Fowler (3900002)	0-4-0DM	1945
Lord Mayor†	402	H/Clarke	0-4-0ST	1839
—	2103	Peckett (2103)	0-4-0ST	1948
—	4200038	Fowler (4200038)	0-4-0DH	1966
—	138C	Thomas Hill (138C)	0-4-0DH	1963

*On loan to the National Railway Museum
†On loan to Keighley & Worth Valley Railway

Stock
Various goods vehicles
5ton Booth rail crane

Owners
1310 (the Steam Power Trust)

Steam centres also play their part in preservation, generally in the provision of locomotives for use over BR metals. Carnforth is one such centre, No 4498 *Sir Nigel Gresley*, currently undergoing major repairs is based there, while No 34092 *City of Wells* is visiting from Keighley prior to working over the main line. *J. H. Cooper-Smith*

North Yorkshire Moors Railway

Headquarters: Pickering station, Pickering, North Yorkshire
Telephone: Pickering (0751) 72508 or 73535
Main station: Pickering
Other public stations: Grosmont, Goathland, Newtondale Halt, Levisham
Car parks: Grosmont, Goathland, Levisham, Pickering
Access by public transport: BR service to Grosmont through tickets available from Whitby and Middlesbrough. United bus services Malton-Pickering, York or Scarborough-Pickering and Whitby-Goathland and Pickering
Refreshment facilities: Available on most trains and at Grosmont, Goathland and Pickering
Souvenir shops: Pickering, Goathland, Grosmont
Museum: Situated within gallery of locomotive depot at Grosmont
Depot: Grosmont
Passenger trains: Diesel and steam-hauled services Grosmont and Pickering (full length 18 miles). Mainly steam during peak holiday season

The 'North Yorkshire Pullman' runs regularly throughout the operating season on Wednesday evenings, it is also available by request on other days. A GWR saloon is also available for special occasions (eg wedding parties, conferences etc)
Period of public operation: Daily Easter-October, with reduced services in early and late season. Santa specials, the three Sundays before Christmas
Facilities for disabled: The NYMR welcomes visitors who may be suffering from a disability and special attention will gladly be provided if advanced notice is given
Special notes: Operates through North York Moors National Park. Information office at Pickering station.
Feature article references: RW December 1982 p646

Locomotives

Name	No	Origin	Class	Type	Built
—	80135	BR	4MT	2-6-4T	1956
Eric Treacy	45428	LMS	5MT	4-6-0	1937
*George Stephenson**	44767	LMS	5MT	4-6-0	1947
—	2238	NER	T2	0-8-0	1918
—	2392	NER	P3	0-6-0	1923
—	2005	LNER	K1	2-6-0	1949
—	69023	LNER	J72	0-6-0T	1951
—	6619	GWR	5600	0-6-2T	1928
Greene King	841	SR	S15	4-6-0	1936
Sidmouth	34010	SR	WC	4-6-2	1945
—	75014	BR	4MT	4-6-0	1951
—	92134	BR	9F	2-10-0	1957
—	63460	NER	T3	0-8-0	1919
Greyhound	D821	BR	42	B-B	1960
—	D2207	BR	03	0-6-0D	1953
—	D5032	BR	24	Bo-Bo	1959
—	D8568	BR	17	Bo-Bo	1963
—	D7029	BR	35	B-B	1962
—	D9520	BR	14	0-6-0DH	1964
—	D9529	BR	14	0-6-0DH	1964
Alycidon	55.009	BR	55	Co-Co	1961
Royal Highland Fusilier	55.019	BR	55	Co-Co	1961

Also dmu vehicles — 4 Glouster RCW (50341, 51118, 56097, 56099) and 3 Swindon-built (79443, 59098, 59099) coaches
*Not on site

NER 0-8-0 No 2238 heads away from Goathland bound for Pickering. *R. D. Clarke*

Industrial locomotives

Name	No	Builder	Type	Built
Mirvale	1	H/Clarke (1882)	0-4-0ST	1955
Meteor	31	RSH (7609)	0-6-0T	1950
Moorbarrow	47	RSH (7849)	0-6-0ST	1955
—	29	Kitson	0-6-2T	1904
—	5	R/Stephenson	0-6-2T	1909
Stanton No 44	—	Yorkshire (2622)	0-4-0DE	1956
No 21	—	Fowler (4210094)	0-4-0DH	1954
Antwerp	—	Hunslet (3180)	0-6-0ST	1944
—	—	E/Electric (1553)	0-6-0DE	1948

Stock
There are 56 coaching stock vehicles on the line comprising 32 Mk 1s, 3 Pullmans and the remainder of 'vintage' category. The 7 pre-Grouping vehicles including NER, H&BR, GNR and GCR examples. There are 14 LNER vehicles including 7 of Edward Thompson design — the largest collection in the country of this CM&EE. The 38 freight vehicles are on the NYMR include several rare or unique examples.

Owners
841 (Essex Locomotive Society)
2005, 2238, 2392, 69023 (the North Eastern Locomotive Preservation Group)
63460 (on loan from the National Railway Museum)
75014 (75014 Locomotive Operators Group)
92134 (the Standard Nine Loco Group)
Antwerp (the National Coal Board)
D821, D7029, D8568 (Diesel Traction Group)
55.009, 55.019 (the Deltic Preservation Society)
21, 44 (British Steel Corporation)
29 (Lambton 29 Syndicate)

Tanfield Railway

Location: Off the A6076 Sunniside to Stanley road
Operating society/organisation: The Tanfield Railway, Marley Hill Engine Shed, Sunniside, Gateshead, Tyne & Wear. Postal address: 33 Stocksfield Avenue, Newcastle-upon-Tyne NE5 2DX
Telephone: Newcastle (091) 2742002
Car park: Marley Hill Engine Shed
Access by public transport: Buses 703-704 from Marlborough bus station, Newcastle, near the Central station pass the railway. Alight at Andrewshouse
On site facilities: Refreshments, shop and toilets
Length of line: 1-mile
Public opening: Marley Hill Engine Shed open every Sunday, trains operate on Bank Holiday Sunday and Mondays from Easter through to August, also every Sunday in June, July and August
Facilities for disabled: Good access to stations
Special notes: The railway is extending its line back to East Tanfield, and is the oldest existing railway in the world, opened in 1725. Also features the Tyneside Locomotive Museum

Stock
10 4-wheel carriages
1 6-wheel carriage
1 6-wheel van
9 hopper wagons
6 contractors bogies
2 brake vans
1 steam crane
6 covered wagons
2 open wagons
1 black wagon

Industrial locomotives

Name	*No*	*Builder*	*Type*	*Built*
—	2502/7	Bagnall (2779)	0-6-0ST	1945
Horden	—	A/Barclay (1015)	0-6-0ST	1904
—	6	A/Barclay (1193)	0-4-2ST	1910
—	17	A/Barclay (1338)	0-6-0T	1913
—	32	A/Barclay (1659)	0-4-0ST	1920
—	3	E. Borrows (37)	0-4-0WT	1898
Wellington	—	B/Hawthorn (266)	0-4-0ST	1873
Enterprise	—	R&W Hawthorn (2009)	0-4-0ST	1884
Cyclops	—	H/Leslie (2711)	0-4-0ST	1907
—	2	H/Leslie (2859)	0-4-0ST	1911
Stagshaw	—	H/Leslie (3513)	0-6-0ST	1923
—	3	H/Leslie (3575)	0-6-0ST	1923
Huncoat No 3	—	H/Leslie (3746)	0-6-0F	1929
Coronation	—	H/Clarke (1672)	0-4-0ST	1937
—	38	H/Clarke (1823)	0-6-0T	1949
—	4	Sentinel (9559)	0-4-0T	1953
Hendon	—	RSH (7007)	0-4-0CT	1940
—	62	RSH (7035)	0-6-0ST	1940
—	49	RSH (7098)	0-6-0ST	1943
Sir Cecil A. Cochrane	—	RSH (7409)	0-4-0ST	1948
—	44	RSH (7760)	0-6-0ST	1953
—	38	RSH (7763)	0-6-0ST	1954
—	21	RSH (7796)	0-4-0ST	1954
—	16	RSH (7944)	0-6-0ST	1957
FGF	—	A/Barclay (552)	0-4-0DH	1969
—	2	A/Whitworth (D22)	0-4-0DE	1933

No 21 running round at Sunniside.
E. Maxwell

WELSH MARCHES EXPRESS
6000

Above:
Steam returned to BR metals in 1971 when No 6000 *King George V* ran a series of trial specials to see whether steam operation was practicable. Each year now sees a considerable number of steam-hauled trips, mainly organised by the Steam Locomotive Operators Association. No 6000 is one of the locomotives currently 'passed' for main line operation, and seen here at the head of the 'Welsh Marches Express'.
C. Milner

Below:
The film industry has made considerable use of preserved lines to provide authenticity to films, television programmes etc. The best known of which is 'The Railway Children' which was filmed on the Keighley & Worth Valley Railway. Another film 'Yanks' made use of the line's American 2-8-0 locomotive seen here. *L. A. Nixon*

Yorkshire Dales Railway

Location: Embsay station, Embsay, Skipton, Yorkshire
Operating society/organisation: Yorkshire Dales Railway Museum Trust
Telephone: Skipton 4727
Car park: Embsay
Access by public transport: West Yorkshire bus routes Nos 75 or 76 from Skipton
On site facilities: Souvenir shop — specialising in transport and industrial archaeological titles, plus model railway supplies, buffet, small museum, real ale saloon on trains
Public opening: Trains run 11.30-dusk on 1 January; 11.00-16.30 on 20-24, 29 April; 6, 7, 13, 20, 27-29 May; 3, 10, 17, 24 June; 1-6, 8, 10, 15, 17, 22, 24, 29, 31 July; 4, 5, 7, 12, 14, 19, 21, 26-28 August; 2, 9, 16, 23, 30 September; 3 November; 9, 16, 23 December. Series 1 Land Rover Rally 29 April; Historic Vehicle Rally 17 June; Good Food and Folk Dance Festival 4, 5 August; Enthusiasts Day 30 September
Special notes: Steam rides are on 1½ miles of track, to be extended in stages. Old Midland Rly buildings, vintage 1896 saloon, fine collection of industrial locomotives

Stock
NER director's saloon coach
5 ex-BR Mk1 coaches
1 ex-BR suburban coach
4 ex-LNER coaches
2 SR parcels vans
Several freight vehicles

Locomotives

Name	*No*	*Origin*	*Class*	*Type*	*Built*
* —	48151	LMS	8F	2-8-0	1942
—	D2203	BR	04	0-6-0DM	195?

***Note:** This locomotive is currently under restoration off site

Industrial locomotives

Name	*No*	*Builder*	*Type*	*Built*
Dorothy	—	H/Clarke (1450)	0-6-0ST	1922
Slough Estates No 5	—	H/Clarke (1709)	0-6-0ST	1939
Primrose No 2	—	Hunslet (3715)	0-6-0ST	1952
Foleshill	—	Peckett (2085)	0-4-0ST	1948
Ann	—	Sentinel (7232)	4wVB	1927
Beatrice	S119	Hunslet (2705)	0-6-0ST	1945
Airedale	—	Hunslet (1440)	0-6-0ST	1923
City Link	—	Yorkshire (2474)	0-4-0ST	1949
—	140	H/Clarke (1821)	0-6-0T	1948
Spitfire	S112	Hunslet (2414)	0-6-0ST	1942
Wheldale	—	Hunslet (3168)	0-6-0T	1944
—	69	Hunslet (3785)	0-6-0ST	1953
Monkton No 1	—	Hunslet (3788)	0-6-0ST	1953
—	22	Barclay (2320)	0-4-0ST	1952
Thomas	4	RSH (7661)	0-4-0ST	1950
H. W. Robinson	—	Fowler (4100003)	0-4-0DM	1946
Darfield No 1	—	Hunslet (3783)	0-6-0ST	1953
—	MDE15	Baguley/Drewry (2136)	4wDM	1938
—	887	Ruston Hornsby (394009)	4wDM	1955
—	—	Wickham (7610)	2w-2PMR	1957
—	—	Lister (9993)*	4wPM	1938
—	—	Lister (10225)*	4wPM	1938
—	—	R/Hornsby*	4wDM	—
—	—	R/Hornsby*	4wDM	—
—	—	M/Rail (8979)*	4wDM	1946
—	—	M/Rail*	4wDM	1930
King Tut†	—	Smith (—)	2-4-2	1932
Annie	—	Peckett (1159)	0-4-0ST	1908
—	—	R/Hornsby	4wDM	1957

* 2ft gauge
† 9½in gauge

A line-up of motive power on the Yorkshire Dales Railway headed by *Slough Estates No 5*. *P. Hatherley*

South Tynedale Railway

Location: Approximately ¼ mile north of Alston town centre, on A686 Hexham road
Operating society: South Tynedale Railway Preservation Society, The Railway Station, Alston, Cumbria CA9 3JB
Telephone: Alston (0498) 81696
Car park: Alston station
Access by public transport: Ribble bus No 681 Haltwhistle station-Alston; Wright Bros bus No 888 Newcastle-Alston-Keswick
On site facilities: Book and souvenir shop, tourist information centre, refreshments, picnic area, toilets (including disabled persons)
Public opening: Alston station open to visitors daily. Passenger train service on 2ft gauge line from Alston to Gilderdale Halt (approx 1½ miles) at Easter weekend, weekends in May and daily June-September
Special notes: The 2ft gauge line has been constructed on the trackbed of the former BR Haltwhistle-Alston branch. Extension of the line from Gilderdale to Slaggyford, a further 3 miles, is planned

Stock
2 bogie coaches
1 brake van
1 bogie box van
2 bogie open wagons
1 4-wheel open wagon
1 fuel tank wagon

Owners
2, 3 and 4 — the Durham Narrow Gauge Group

Locomotives

Name	*No*	*Builder*	*Type*	*Built*
—	1	Hibberd (2325)	4wDM	1937
Ayle	2	Hudson-Hunslet (2607)	4wDM	1942
Sao Domingos	3	O/Koppel (11784)	0-6-0WT	1925
—	4	H/Clarke (DM819)	0-6-0DM	1952
—	5	Simplex (11297)	4wDM	1964

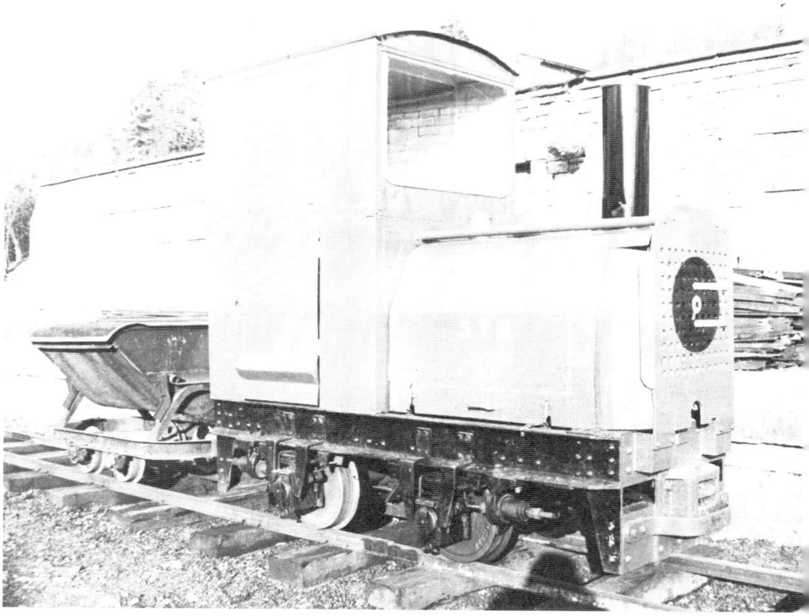

Restored Hibberd diesel and skip at Alston station.
A. Chambers

Beamish

Location: North of England Open Air Museum, near Stanley, County Durham
Telephone: Stanley (0207) 31811
Car park: At museum site
Access by public transport: Bus service No 704 from Marlborough Crescent, Newcastle upon Tyne; Bus service No 775 from Market Place, Chester-le-Street
On site facilities: 200 acre open air museum showing the past way of life of the people of the North East. Home Farm, Colliery with furnished pit cottages, Railway area with station, signal box and goods shed. Transport collection. Tram rides and locos often in steam. Tea Room and Victorian pub (summer only)

Nos 876 and 14 seen outside the goods shed. The former Rowley station was re-erected at Beamish. *J. Gotts*

For the past nine years the ARPS has sponsored an annual award which is given to the society which has done the most to epitomise what preservation is all about. The first winner, in 1975, was the Great Western Society who repeated their success in 1981. One of the reasons for the award was due to the fact that they had restored to main line running a complete rake of Great Western coaches. The final run of the train was on 26 January 1980 behind their newly restored No 5051 *Drysllwyn Castle*. *G. Lockley*

Public opening: April-mid-September: Daily 10.00-18.00. Locos not in steam after 16.00. Mid-September-March 10.00-17.00, closed Mondays. No locos in steam. Last admission is always one hour before closing time
Length of line: Approx ½-mile single line connecting rebuilt NER station to colliery sidings. No through passenger trains
Facilities for disabled: Special passes available at main entrance to permit cars to drive round the site. Wheelchair access to Hall, Visitor Centre and station. Disabled toilets at two locations but not station. No wheelchair access to Tearoom but snack bar accessible. Rolling stock not converted but special arrangements possible. Advanced notice for parties to Booking Clerk preferred

Locomotives

Name	*No*	*Origin*	*Class*	*Type*	*Built*
—	876	NER	C1	0-6-0	1889
Locomotion	1*	—	—	0-4-0	1975

*Replica

Industrial Locomotives

Name	*No*	*Builder*	*Type*	*Built*
Twizell	3	Stephenson (2730)	0-6-0T	1891
—	14	H/Leslie (3056)	0-4-0ST	1914
South Durham Malleable	No 5	Stockton Ironworks	0-4-0ST	c1880
—	—	Head Wrightson	0-4-0VB	1871
—	18	Lewin	0-4-0WT	1863
—	E1	Black, Hawthorn	2-4-0CT	1883
Hetton Loco	—	G. Stephenson	0-4-0	1822
—	—	R/Hornsby (476140)	0-4-0DM	1963

Owner
Hetton Loco (on loan from National Railway Museum

Bowes Railway

Location: Bowes Railway, Springwell Village, near Gateshead, Tyne & Wear. (on B1288 at OS Grid Ref NZ 285589)
Operating society/organisation: Bowes Railway Co Ltd
Telephone: Washington 4161847 (Railway)/Newcastle 816144 (Regd Office)
Car park: Springwell
Access by public transport: Northern Buses services Nos 181 Chester-le-Street/ Washington, 183 Newcastle/Rickington, 188 Newcastle/Sunderland, 189 Newcastle/Washington, 638 Sunderland/ Ryton. Buses from Newcastle leave Worswick St bus station and call at Gateshead Metro interchange
On site facilities: Exhibition of Railway's history, wagon exhibition, workshop displays, visitors trail. On operating days — Shop, refreshments and guided tours. Steam hauled brake van rides. Rope haulage demonstration trains
Public opening: Static, weekdays 10.00-16.00 (report to manager's offices, weekends 10.30-16.00
Operational: First Sunday in month from Easter to October. Also bank holiday Sunday and Monday. Admission and car park free. 11.00-14.30 (last train)
Length of line: 1¾ miles total length; 1½ miles of rope haulage; ¾ mile used for passenger trains
Special notes: Preserved section of the Pontop and Jarrow Railway; designed G. Stephenson; opened 1826; Only standard gauge rope-hauled incline railway in preservation; Railway's own historic workshops preserved, with examples of most of the railway's wagons

Industrial locomotives

Name	*No*	*Builder*	*Type*	*Bulit*
WST	—	Barclay (2361)	0-4-0ST	1954
Area No 85	22	Barclay (2274)	0-4-0ST	1949
Norwood	—	RSH (7412)	0-6-0ST	1948
—	101	Planet (3922)	4wDM	1959
—	—	Smith (18773)	4wCT	1948

Owners
Area No 85 (On loan from Thomas Ness Ltd)
WST (On loan from British Gypsum Ltd)
Norwood (On loan from National Smokeless Fuels)

Stock
21 Ordinary 10 ton wooden hopper wagons (Springwell built)
16 other wooden hopper wagons (of various pedigrees)
1 steel 14-ton hopper wagon
1 reel bogie (for rope replacement)
1 drift bogie (for shunting by rope)
1 loco coal wagon
4 material wagons
1 tool van
3 brake vans
2 flat wagons

Stationary haulage
Met-Vick/Wild, 300bhp (Blackham's Hill) 1950
BTH/Robey, 500bhp (Black Fell) 1950
Clarke Chapman, 22hp (Springwell Yard)
14ft Diam, Gravity Dilly Wheel (Springwell)

Darlington Railway Museum

Location: North Road station, Darlington, County Durham DL3 6ST
Telephone: 0325 460532
Car park: At museum site
Access by public transport: BR services (not Sundays) to Darlington North Road station. Also good local bus service
On site facilities: Souvenir shop. Light refreshments available
Public opening: Monday-Saturday from 10.00-17.00 (Easter-September)
10.00-15.00 (October-Easter)
Sundays 11.00-16.00 (Easter-September). Subject to possible amendment during 1984

Locomotives

Name	*No*	*Origin*	*Class*	*Type*	*Built*
Locomotion	1	S&DR	—	0-4-0	1825
Derwent	25	S&DR	—	0-6-0	1845
—	1275	NER	—	0-6-0	1874
—	1463	NER	—	2-4-0	1885

Industrial locomotives

Name	*No*	*Builder*	*Type*	*Built*
Met	—	H/Leslie (2800)	0-4-0ST	1909
—	17	Head Wrightson (33)	0-4-0VB	1873
—	—	Bagnall (2898)	0-4-0F	1948

Stock
1 Stockton & Darlington Rly passenger coach
1 North Eastern Railway Coach body (c1860)
1 NER 20ton mineral wagon
1 Chaldron wagon

Owners
Locomotion, Derwent and Nos 1275 and 1463 are all on loan from the National Railway Museum

National Railway Museum

Location: National Railway Museum, Leeman Road, York YO2 4XJ
Operating society/organisation: Part of the Science Museum, London
Telephone: York 21261 (STD Code 0904)
Car park: Limited parking for cars and coaches at the Museum. Prior booking is necessary for coaches
Access by public transport: The Museum is within a few minutes' walking distance of the railway and bus stations in York. The York-West Yorkshire Bus Service operates to the door
On site facilities: Museum shop and refreshments

The former York motive power depot now forms part of the NRM's complex. LSWR No 563 nearest the camera.
A. C. Butcher

Public opening: Daily, weekdays 10.00-18.00. Sundays 14.30-18.00. Closed on some public holidays

Special notes: York is a centre for 'Steam on BR' steam-hauled railtours over BR main lines. The Museum's collection is an extensive one, and there are three or four times as many items as can be exhibited in the Museum at one time. Various items are loaned to other museums and preservation societies, details of which appear in the appropriate entry. Others are 'rotated' between the Museum and the reserve collection in the Peter Allen Building. Within the currency of *Railways Restored 1984*, therefore, it is not possible to indicate exactly which locomotives, carriages and wagons will be on display in the Museum, but Table 1 indicates those items which form the first choice for public exhibition. For completeness the other items expected to be located at York are given in Table 2, but it is unlikely that any of these will be on public display in the immediate future. It must be emphasised, therefore, that the appearance of any particular item on public display cannot be guaranteed, but if it is vital for anyone to discover whether a specific locomotive or vehicle is on exhibition, they should contact the museum beforehand. The Museum attracts some 1 million visitors a year, and is generally less crowded during the winter months

Feature article references: RW January 1982 p6; RW August 1982 p412

TABLE 1

Locomotives

Name	*No*	*Origin*	*Builder*	*Class*	*Type*	*Built*
Agenoria	—	Pensnett Railway	Foster, Rastrick	—	0-4-0	1829
(Columbine)	1868	Grand Junction Railway	Crewe	—	2-2-2	1845
Coppernob	3	Furness Railway	Bury Curtis & Kennedy	—	0-4-0	1846
Aerolite	66	NER	Gateshead	XI(LNER)	2-2-4T	1869
—	No 1	GNR	Doncaster	A2	4-2-2	1870
—	910	NER	Gateshead	901	2-4-0	1875
Boxhill	82	LBSCR	Brighton	A1	0-6-0T	1880
Gladstone	214	LBSCR	Brighton	B1	0-4-2	1882
Wren	—	LYR	B/Peacock	—	0-4-0ST (1ft 6in gauge)	1887
—	1008	LYR	Horwich	—	2-4-2T	1889
Hardwicke	790	LNWR	Crewe	—	2-4-0	1892
—	1621	NER	Gateshead	M	4-4-0	1893
—	563	LSWR	Nine Elms	T3	4-4-0	1893
—	75S	Waterloo & City	Siemens (6)	—	4wE	1898
—	673	MR	Derby	—	4-2-2	1899
—	1247	GNR	S/Stewart (4492)	J52	0-6-0ST	1899
—	251	GNR	Doncaster	C1	4-4-2	1902
—	1000	MR	Derby	4	4-4-0	1902
—	87	GER	Stratford	P57	0-6-0T	1904
—	1	NER	BTH/Brush	—	Bo-Bo	1904
—	2818	GWR	Swindon	2800	2-8-0	1905
[1] —	K1	Tasmanian Railways	B/Peacock (5292)	—	0-4-0+0-4-0 (1ft 11½in gauge)	1909
[2] —	7401	LMS	Hunslet (1697)		0-6-0DM	1932
[3] —	607	Chinese National Railways	Vulcan	KF1	4-8-4	1935
Green Arrow	4771	LNER	Doncaster	V2	2-6-2	1936
[4] *Duchess of Hamilton*	46229	LMS	Crewe	Coronation	4-6-2	1938
Mallard	4468	LNER	Doncaster	A4	4-6-2	1938
Winston Churchill	34051	SR	Brighton	BB	4-6-2	1946
**Ellerman Lines*	35029	SR	Eastleigh	MN	4-6-2	1949
—	—	Teeside Bridge & Eng Co	Sentinel (9629)	4wTG	1957	
Imperial Paper Mills	1	Imperial Paper Mills, Gravesend	A/Barclay (2375)		0-4-0F	1956
Evening Star	92220	BR	Swindon	9F	2-10-0	1960
—	D2860	BR	YEC	02	0-4-0DH	1960
The Kings Own Yorkshire Light Infantry	55.002	BR	E/Electric	55	Co-Co	1961
Rocket (reproduction)	L&MR	Locomotion Enterprises	—	—	0-2-2	1979

Electric Motor Coaches

Name	No	Origin	Builder	Class/Type	Built
—	28249	LNWR	—	Driving Motor 3rd	1915
—	8143	SR	—	Driving Motor 3rd	1925

[1] On loan from Festiniog Railway
[2] On loan from Middleton Railway
[3] A gift to the NRM from the Chinese Ministry of Railways
[4] On loan from Butlins Ltd
*Sectioned exhibit

TABLE 2

Locomotives

Name	No	Origin	Builder	Class	Type	Built
[5] *Hodbarrow*	1	—	Hunslet (299)	—	0-4-0ST	1882
—	490	GER	Stratford	T26	2-4-0	1894
—	245	LSWR	Nine Elms	M7	0-4-4T	1897
Henry Oakley	990	GNR	Doncaster	C2	4-4-2	1898
—	737	SECR	Ashford	D	4-4-0	1901
Sir Lamiel	777	SR	N/British	KA	4-6-0	1925
—	2700	LMS	Horwich	5P4F	2-6-0	1926
Cheltenham	925	SR	Eastleigh	V	4-4-0	1934
—	—	Yorkshire Water Authority	R/Hornsby (187105)	—	4wDM (2ft gauge)	1937
Eustace Forth	15	CEGB	RSH (7063)	—	0-4-0ST	1942
—	No 3	CEGB	RSH(7746)	—	0-6-0DM	1954
—	20.050	BR	E/Electric	20	Bo-Bo	1957
—	D5500	BR	Brush	31	AIA-AIA	1958
—	E5001	BR	Doncaster	71	Bo-Bo	1958
—	03.090	BR	Doncaster	03	0-6-0DM	1960
[6] —	84.001	BR	N/British	84	Bo-Bo	1960

Electric Motor Coaches

—	11179	SR	—	Driving Motor 3rd	1937
—	PC1 & 2	BR	Derby	APTE Artic	1972

[5] On loan from Hunslet Engine Co
[6] On loan from BR

Diesel Traction Group

Location: North Yorkshire Moors Railway (BREL Swindon Works)
Operating society/organisation: Diesel Traction Group, 28 Talma Gardens, Twickenham, Middlesex
Public opening: During NYMR operating season (on special works open days)
Special notes: D1015 is stored on BREL property and is therefore not available for public viewing. It can however be seen from passing trains.

Locomotives

Name	No	Origin	Class	Type	Built
*Greyhound**	D821	BR	42	B-B	1960
—*	D7029	BR	35	B-B	1962
Western Champion	D1015	BR	52	C-C	1962
—*	D8568	BR	17	Bo-Bo	1963

*Located on NYMR

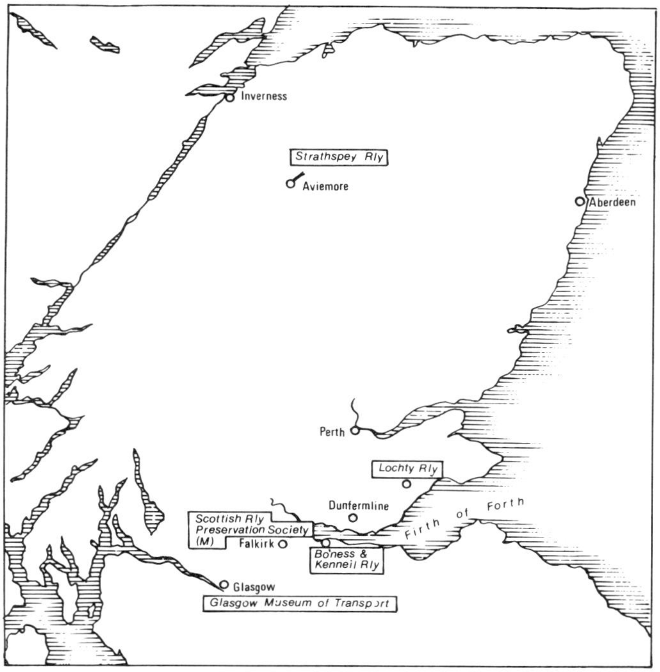

Strathspey Railway

Headquarters: The Station, Boat of Garten, Inverness-shire PH24 3BH
Telephone: 047 983 692
Main station: Boat of Garten
Other public stations: Aviemore
Car parks: Aviemore and Boat of Garten
Access by public transport: BR services to Aviemore. Highland buses to Boat of Garten
Refreshment facilities: On train buffet car
Souvenir shop: Boat of Garten
Museum: Boat of Garten
Depot: Aviemore (not generally open to public)
Passenger trains: Steam-hauled services. Boat of Garten-Aviemore (5 miles)
Period of public operation: Weekends from mid May-mid-October. Daily except Thursdays and Fridays from end of June, July and August. Also Easter weekend
Facilities for disabled: Access possible at both stations. But please contact in advance for directions and if a party involved
Special notes: First and third class travel available on most trains. Family fares available for third class travel. Special rates/arrangements for parties. Evening diner trains — for booked parties — phone 047 983 258 for details/bookings

Locomotives

Name	*No*	*Origin*	*Class*	*Type*	*Built*
—	5025	LMS	5MT	4-6-0	1934
—	46464	LMS	2MT	2-6-0	1950
—	46512	LMS	2MT	2-6-0	1952
—	828	CR	3F	0-6-0	1899
Schichallion	44.008	BR	44	1Co-Co1	1959

Hunslet 0-6-0ST No 60 departs Boat of Garton with the 14.00 to Aviemore. *D. M. May*

Stock
10 ex-BR coaches
5 ex-LMS coaches
1 Pullman coach
3 ex-LMS sleeping cars
1 ex-LNER sleeping car
1 ex-LNWR coach
1 ex-HR coach
1 ex-NBR coach
2 ex-GNSR coaches
Numerous examples of rolling stock

Industrial locomotives

Name	*No*	*Builder*	*Type*	*Built*
—	48	Hunslet (2864)	0-6-0ST	1943
Cairngorm	9	RSH (7097	0-6-0ST	1943
—	60	Hunslet (3686)	0-6-0ST	1948
*Forth**	10	Barclay (1890)	0-4-0ST	1926
Dailuaine	1	Barclay (2073)	0-4-0ST	1939
Balmenach	2	Barclay (2020)	0-4-0ST	1936
—	7	Barclay (2017)	0-6-0T	1935
Clyde	3	Barclay (2315)	0-4-0ST	1951
Inveresk	14	R/Hornsby (260756)	0-4-0DM	1950
Madelene	18	R/Hornsby (304471)	0-4-0DM	1951
Inverdon	15	Simplex (5763)	4wDM	1957
—	16	North British (27549)	0-4-0DM	1951
Niddrie	6	Barclay (1833)	0-6-0ST	1924
Queen Anne	20	R/Hornsby (265618)	4wDM	1948

*Not on site

Owners
46512 (the Highland Locomotive Co Ltd)
46464 (Dundee City Museum)
828 (the Scottish Locomotive Preservation Trust Fund)

Bo'ness & Kinneil Railway

Location: Scottish Railway Preservation Society, Bo'ness Station, Union Street, Bo'ness, West Lothian, EH51
Telephone: Bo'ness 822298
Main station: Bo'ness
Car park: At the site
Refreshment facilities: Bo'ness
Souvenir shops: Bo'ness
Depot: Bo'ness
Passenger trains: Trains run at regular intervals in season on Saturdays, Sundays 12.00-17.00hrs incl
Length of line: Almost $\frac{1}{2}$ mile
Period of public operation: Easter-September and Christmas
Facilities for disabled: At Bo'ness for shop and cafeteria
Feature article references: RW June 1982 p353

Locomotives

Name	*No*	*Origin*	*Class*	*Type*	*Built*
—	1313	SJ	B	4-6-0	1917
—	419	CR	439	0-4-4T	1907

Industrial locomotives

Name	*No*	*Builder*	*Type*	*Built*
Clydesmill Power Station	3	Barclay (1937)	0-4-0ST	1928
—	24	Barclay (2355)	0-6-0T	1953
Sir John King	—	H/Leslie (3640)	0-4-0ST	1926
D7 Pioneer	—	R/Hornsby (275883)	4wDM	1949
—	P6687	R/Hornsby (312984)	0-4-0DE	1951

Stock
A selection of coaches and wagons

Owners
24 (owned by Royal Scottish Museum)

Lochty Railway

Headquarters: Balbuthie, Leven, Fife
Telephone: St Monace 210
Main station: Lochty
Car park: Lochty
Access by public transport: Nearest bus service; St Andrews-Anstruther service ($1\frac{3}{4}$ mile walk)
Souvenir shop: Lochty
Passenger trains: Steam-hauled from Lochty through the estate of J. B. Cameron ($1\frac{1}{2}$ miles)
Period of public operation: Operates only on Sundays from 14.00. Mid-June till first Sunday in September

Locomotive

Name	*No*	*Origin*	*Class*	*Type*	*Built*
Union of South Africa	60009	LNER	A4	4-6-2	1937

Industrial locomotives

Name	*No*	*Builder*	*Type*	*Built*
—	1	Peckett (1376)	0-4-0ST	1915
—	16	Bagnall (2759)	0-6-0ST	1944
—	—	R/Hornsby (421415)	4wDM	1958

Note:
No 60009 *Union of South Africa* is stored at Markinch station for main line use on railtours.

Special notes: This, Britain's shortest standard gauge railway, operates entirely through the property of J. B. Cameron and no statutory authority was required in order to permit commencement of services in 1967

Stock
1 ex-BR Mk 1 coach
1 LNER observation coach
1 ex-NBR 8ton box van (built 1901)
8 assorted private owner wagons

Scottish Railway Preservation Society (Falkirk Depot)

Location: Scottish Railway Preservation Society, Springfield Yard, off Wallace Street, Falkirk FK2 7DR
Operating society/organisation: Scottish Railway Preservation Society
Telephone: Falkirk 20790
Car park: At the Site
On site facilities: Souvenir shop and refreshments
Public opening: Static displays at weekends
Special notes: The society promotes a number of railtours originating in the Scottish Region of BR

Locomotives

Name	*No*	*Origin*	*Class*	*Type*	*Built*
—	80105	BR	4MT	2-6-4T	1955
Morayshire	246	LNER	D49	4-4-0	1928
Maude	673	NBR	—	0-6-0	1891
—	D9524	BR	14	0-6-0DH	1964

Industrial locomotives

Name	*No*	*Builder*	*Type*	*Built*
—	3	Barclay (1458)	0-6-0ST	1916
The Wemyss Coal Co Ltd	20	Barclay (2068)	0-6-0T	1939
—	6	Barclay (2127)	0-4-0CT	1942
Borrowstouness	—	Barclay (840)	0-4-0T	1899 (3ft 0in gauge)
—	D180/001	Barclay (343)	0-6-0DM	1941
City of Aberdeen	—	B/Hawthorn (912)	0-4-0ST	1887
Flash	—	E/Electric (701)	6wBE	1926
F82 (Fairfield)	—	E/Electric (1131)	4wBE	1940
Ellesmere	—	Hawthorns (Leith) (244)	0-4-0WT	1861
Kelton Fell	13	Neilson (2203)	0-4-0ST	1876
NCB Lord Roberts	1	Neilson/Reid (5710)	0-6-0T	1902
—	D88/001	R/Hornsby (262998)	4wDM	1949

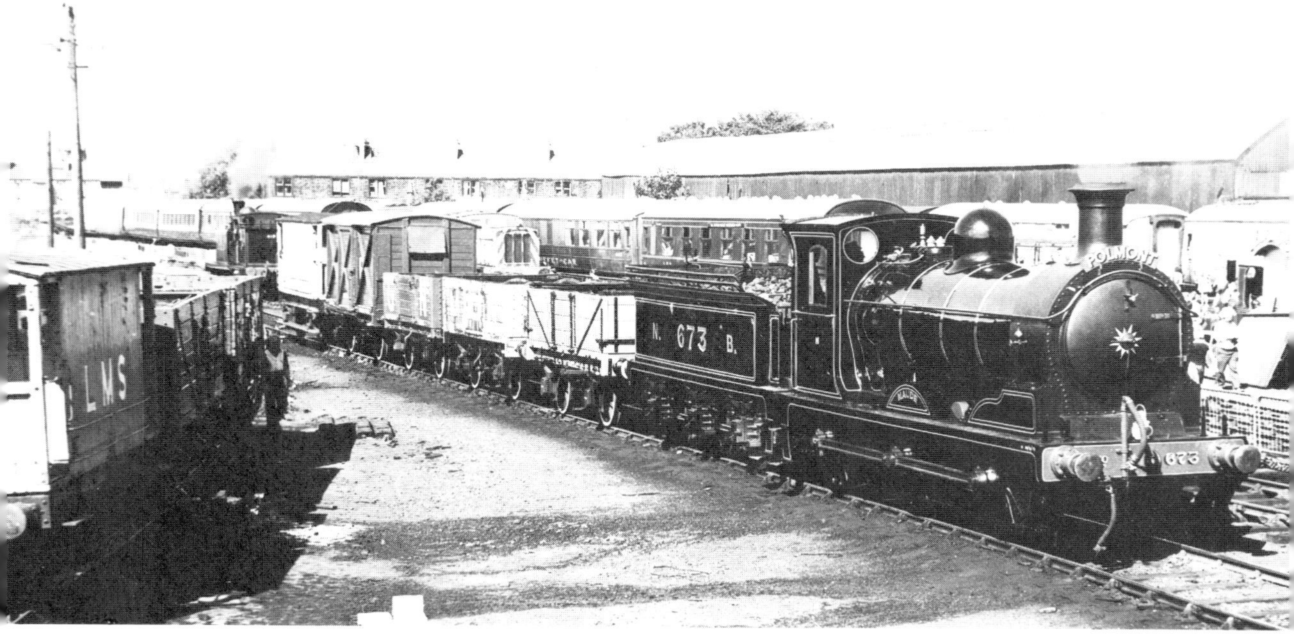

NBR 0-6-0 No 673 *Maude* with a selection of rolling stock at Falkirk. *S. Sellar*

Name	No	Builder	Type	Built
—	1	R/Hornsby (421439)	0-4-0DE	1958
—	3	R/Hornsby (423658)	0-4-0DE	1958
—	D88/003	R/Hornsby (506500)	4wDM	1965
Diesel No 3	—	R/Hornsby	0-4-0DE	1958
—		(423662)		
—	—	BTH	4wE	1908
Oakbank Oil Co Ltd No 2	—	Baldwin (20587)	4wE	1902 (2ft 6in gauge)

Stock
A large selection of coaching stock, many built by Scottish pre-Grouping companies, and an appropriate collection of early freight vehicles

Owners
80105 (owned by Scottish Locomotive Owners Group)
246 (owned by Royal Scottish Museum)

Glasgow Museum of Transport

Location: 25 Albert Drive, Glasgow G41 2PE
Operating society/organisation: City of Glasgow District Council, Museums & Art Galleries Department
Telephone: 041-423-8000
Car park: Street parking available nearby
Access by public transport: Pollokshields East station; Strathclyde PTE bus service No 59 and others
On site facilities: Souvenir shop and tea room
Public opening: Weekdays including Saturdays 10.00-17.00, Sundays 14.00-17.00. Including public holidays except 1 January and 25 December
Facilities for disabled: Access available to all displays and facilities. No advance notice required
Special notes: Admission free

Locomotives

Name	No	Origin	Class	Type	Built
—	123	CR	123	4-2-2	1866
—	9	G&SWR	5	0-6-0T	1917
—	103	HR	—	4-6-0	1894
Glen Douglas	256	NBR	K	4-4-0	1913
Gordon Highlander	49	GNSR	F	4-4-0	1920

Industrial locomotives

Name	No	Builder	Type	Built
—	1	Barclay (1571)	0-6-0F	1917
—	—	Chaplin (2368)	0-4-0TG	1888

Stock
1 Glasgow District Subway car No 39T
1 Glasgow Corporation Underground car No 12

Prestongrange Mining Museum

Location: Main coast road between Musselburgh and Prestonpans, 7½ miles east of Edinburgh
Operating society/organisation: East Lothian District Council. Details c/o Hon Curator, David Spence, 24 Woodlands Grove, Edinburgh EH15 3PP
Car park: On site
On site facilities: Refreshments and engines in steam first Sunday of month April-October
Public opening: Caretaker on site all year round except Saturdays. Parties can be arranged through Curator. Visitors welcome on Sundays when volunteers are at work
Special notes: Artifacts and documents on display

Isle of Man Railway

Headquarters: Isle of Man Railways, Terminus Building, Strathallan Crescent, Douglas, Isle of Man
Telephone: Douglas 4549
Main station: Douglas
Other public stations: Port Soderick, Castletown, Port Erin, Ballasalla, Port St Mary
Car parks: Douglas, Ballasalla, Castletown, Port Erin
Access by public transport: Isle of Man Transport buses to main centres
Refreshment facilities: Port Erin
Souvenir shops: Douglas, Port Erin
Museum: Port Erin
Depot: Douglas
Passenger trains: 3ft gauge line Douglas-Port Erin ($15\frac{1}{4}$ miles)
Period of public operation: Sundays to Fridays mid-May to end-September
Facilities for disabled: Level access throughout Douglas and Port Erin stations including snack bar. Carriages able to carry wheelchairs, ramps provided. Advance notice helpful
Special notes: No service operates on Saturdays
Feature article reference: RW January 1983 p27

No 13 *Kissack* leaves Douglas with the 10.10 to Port Erin on 1 June 1983.
D. Percival

Locomotives

Name	No	Builder	Type	Built
Loch	4*	B/Peacock (1416)	2-4-0T	1874
G. H. Wood	10	B/Peacock (4462)	2-4-0T	1905
Maitland	11*	B/Peacock (4463)	2-4-0T	1905
Hutchinson	12*	B/Peacock (5162)	2-4-0T	1908
Kissack	13*	B/Peacock (5382)	2-4-0T	1910
—	19*	Walker (GNR (I))	diesel railcar	1950
—	20*	Walker (GNR (I))	diesel railcar	1951

*Operational, No 10 is stored out of use, not on display.

On display in museum at Port Erin

Name	No	Builder	Type	Built
Sutherland	1	B/Peacock (1253)	2-4-0T	1873
Caledonia	15	Dubs & Co (2178)	0-6-0T	1885
Mannin	16	B/Peacock (6296)	2-4-0T	1926

Owned by Isle of Man Railway Society (not on display)

Name	No	Builder	Type	Built
Mona	5	B/Peacock (1417)	2-4-0T	1874
*Tynwald**	7	B/Peacock (2038)	2-4-0T	1880
Fenella	8	B/Peacock (3610)	2-4-0T	1894
Douglas	9	B/Peacock (3815)	2-4-0T	1896

*Chassis only

Manx Electric Railway

Headquarters: Isle of Man Railways, Terminus Building, Strathallan Crescent, Douglas, Isle of Man
Telephone: Douglas (0624) 4549
Main station: Douglas (Derby Castle)
Other public stations: Laxey, Ramsey
Car parks: Douglas, Laxey, Ramsey nearby
Access by public transport: Isle of Man Transport buses to main centres
Refreshment facilities: Laxey
Museum and souvenirs: Ramsey
Passenger service: 3ft gauge line Douglas-Ramsey
Length of line: 17 miles
Period of public operations: Monday-Friday all year. Saturdays early May-end September. Sundays end May-mid September
Special notes: No special facilities for disabled. Folded wheelchairs can be carried. Please notify in advance

Motor cars

Nos	Type	Seats	Body	Built
1, 2	Unvestibuled saloon	34	Milnes	1893
5, 6, 7, 9	Vestibuled saloon	32	Milnes	1894
14, 15, 17, 18	Cross-bench open	56	Milnes	1898
16	Cross-bench open	56	Milnes	1898
19-22	Winter saloon	48	Milnes	1899
23	Centre-cab locomotive	—	IOMT & EP	1900
25-27	Cross-bench open	56	Milnes	1898
28-31	Cross-bench open	56	ERTCW	1904
32, 33	Cross-bench open	56	UEC	1906

This Manx Electric motor car, No 18, dates from 1898. *A. A. Scarffe*

Trailers

36, 37	Cross-bench open	44	Milnes	1894
40, 41, 44	Cross-bench open	44	EE Co	1930
42, 43	Cross-bench open	44	Milnes	1903
45-48	Cross-bench open	44	Milnes	1899
49-51, 53, 54	Cross-bench open	44	Milnes	1893
52	pw flatcar (ex trailer)	—	Milnes	1893
55, 56	Cross-bench open	44	ERTCW	1904
57, 58	Saloon	32	ERTCW	1904
59	Special Saloon	18	Milnes	1895
60	Cross-bench open	44	Milnes	1896
61, 62	Cross-bench open	44	UEC	1906

Snaefell Mountain Railway

Headquarters: Isle of Man Railways, Terminus Building, Strathallan Crescent, Douglas, Isle of Man
Telephone: Douglas (0624) 4549
Main station: Laxey
Other public stations: Bungalow, Summit
Car parks: Laxey, Bungalow (nearby)
Access by public transport: Manx Electric Railway or National Transport bus to Laxey
Refreshment facilities: Laxey, Summit
Museum: Ramsey
Souvenirs: Summit
Passenger service: 3ft 6in gauge line Laxey-Snaefell summit
Length of line: 5 miles
Period of public operation: Monday-Saturday mid-May to mid-September. Sundays June to mid-September
Special notes: No special facilities for disabled

Nos	*Type*	*Seats*	*Body*	*Built*
1-4, 6	Vestibuled saloon	48	Milnes	1895
5	Vestibuled saloon	48	MER/ Kinnin	1971

Ramsey Electric Railway Museum

Location: Manx Electric Railway Station, Parsonage Road, Ramsey, Isle of Man
Operating society/organisation: (General enquiries) Isle of Man Railway Society, 4 Clifton Road, Rugby, Warwickshire
(Applications for special opening) Mr P. Richardson, 6 King Edward Park, Onchan, Isle of Man
Telephone: (General enquiries) 0788 3026
Car parks: Locally in nearby street
Access by public transport: Manx Electric Railway station adjoins museum; Douglas-Laxey-Ramsey buses pass within a few yards, alight at Parsonage Road
On site facilities: Museum shop, toilets in MER station
Public opening: Sundays to Friday (not Saturdays except by prior arrangement) 11.15am-4.00pm, mid-May-late September

No	*Origin/Type*	*Built*
	Manx Electric Railway	
23	MER Bo-Bo electric loco	1900
26	MER Bogie freight car	1895
59	MER Royal saloon trailer	1895
	Douglas Horse Trams	
11	Douglas, open toastrack	1886
47	Douglas, bulkhead car	1911
49	Douglas, convertible car	1935
—	Horse tram transporter wagon	1930s
	Queens Pier Tramway	
—	Hibberd 'Planet' 4WPM (2037)	1937
—	Hibberd-PRV bogie trailer (2038)	1937

*Trailer 59 is a part of the operational stock of the MER

Special notes: For parties travelling by MER, opening outside normal hours may sometimes be possible. Enquiries should be routed via Mr P. Richardson (address above)

IRELAND

Railway Preservation Society of Ireland

Location: Whitehead Excursion station
Operating society: Railway Preservation Society of Ireland
Telephone: Whitehead (096 033) 78567
Car park: At the site
Access by public transport: Northern Ireland Railways services from Belfast (York Road) or Larne Harbour: Ulster Bus service
On site facilities: Souvenir shop, refreshments in dining car, open on Sundays during June, July and August
Public opening: Sundays during June, July and August for steam train rides and for Santa services on last Sunday of November and December Sundays before 25 December
Special notes: The RPSI is noted for its main line railtours operated each year using its own rolling stock and coaches. For the 1984 season the following railtour dates are provisional: 21 April 'Claddagh Railtour' Mullingar-Galway and return; 22/23 April Easter Bunny train rides at Whitehead; 5 May Whitehead-Mullinger; 12/13/14 May 3 day 'Galway Bay Railtour' Dublin Connolly-Whitehead; 21 July, 4/18 August 'Portrush Flyer' Whitehead-Castlerock and return; 1/15 September 'Steam Enterprise' Belfast-Dublin and return; 23 September 'Larne Lough Railtour' Belfast-Whitehead. For details telephone above number and leave name and address

Steam train rides Sundays in June, July, August 14.00-17.00 at Whitehead. Santa train rides 25 November, 1/2, 9, 16 December 13.30-16.30 at Whitehead
Feature article reference: RW April 1982 p180

Locomotives

Name	No	Origin	Class	Type	Built
Merlin	85	GNR (I)	V	4-4-0	1932
Slieve Gullion	171	GNR (I)	S	4-4-0	1913
—	4	LMS (NCC)	WT	2-6-4T	1947
—	184*	GS&WR	J15	0-6-0	1880
—	186	GS&WR	J15	0-6-0	1879
—	461*	D&SER	K2	2-6-0	1922
Lough Erne	27	SL&NCR	—	0-6-4T	1949

Industrial locomotives

Name	No	Builder	Type	Built
Guinness	3	H/Clarke (1152)	0-4-0ST	1919
R. H. Smyth	3	Avonside (2021)	0-6-0ST	1928
—	23	Planet	0-4-0DM	1951

Stock
The Society also owns some 20 coaches, normally resident at Whitehead, where a small number of freight wagons are also preserved

*Normally based in the Republic of Ireland

No 184 pulls away from Longford with a railtour. *C. P. Freil*

Irish Steam Preservation Society

Location: Stradbally Hall, eight miles from Athy, six miles from Portlaoise.
Operating society/organisation: Irish Steam Preservation Society Ltd, Secretary, Mrs O. Condell, Bay House, Main Street, Stradbally, Co Laois
Telephone: (0502) 25136
Access by public transport: CIE train to Athy or Portlaoise, CIE bus Dublin-Kilkenny route (certain days only)
On site facilities: 3ft gauge railway museum in nearby town

Industrial locomotives

Name	No	Builder	Type	Built
—	—	A/Barclay (2264)	0-4-0WT	1949
—	—	Hunslet (2281)	4wDM	1941

Stock
1 Wickham trolley
1 Passenger coach
1 Ballast wagon

Public opening: Appointments to visit the museum, and details of open days, apply to the above address. 1984 Open days 22/23 April, 3/4 June, 28/29 October. 14.30-17.00 on all dates. 5/6 August (National Traction Engine Rally)

Special notes: 1984 is the 150th anniversary of the Irish railway system. It is hoped the society will be able to share with other societies in the celebrations. Enquiries from groups interested in special workings will be welcome

Shanes Castle Railway

Headquarters: Antrim station, Shanes Castle Estate, Co Antrim, Northern Ireland
Telephone: Antrim 3380/2216
Main station: Antrim (SCR)
Car parks: Shanes Castle Estate, Antrim
Access by public transport: By Ulsterbus from several centres. By NI Railways to Antrim station
Refreshment facilities: Shanes Castle
Souvenir shop: Shanes Castle
Passenger trains: Steam-hauled trains from Antrim station ($1\frac{1}{2}$ miles) through the Shanes Castle estate. Narrow (3ft) gauge railway
Period of public operation: Sundays, April-August. Also Bank Holidays, Wednesdays, Saturdays, July-August. Opening times 13.00-18.00; Bank Holidays 12.00-18.00
Special notes: Railway serves visitors to the Shanes Castle estate of Lord O'Neill which includes an extensive nature reserve

Locomotives

Name	*No*	*Builder*	*Type*	*Built*
Tyrone	1	Peckett (1026)	0-4-0T	1904
Shane	3	Barclay (2265)	0-4-0WT	1949
Nancy	5	Avonside (1547)	0-6-0T	1908
Rory	2	Simplex (11039)	0-4-0DM	1956
Nippy	4	Planet (2014)	0-4-0DM	1936

Stock
12 4-wheel carriages
3 4-wheel Tram cars

In storage
(owned by Dr R. Cox; all ex-Co Donegal Railway)
Nasmyth Wilson (830) 2-6-4T *Columbkille* 1907
Railcar No 12 Walker Bros (1934)
Railcar No 18 GNR(I) (1940)
Carriage No 14 Oldburg
Red Wagon

Barclay 0-4-0WT No 3 *Shane*. *C. P. Freil*

Photo Feature

As mentioned in the introduction 1984 is the 'Year of the Coach', this short photo feature takes a look at this aspect of railway preservation.

Above:
The Didcot Railway Centre has constructed a building to deal with the restoration of its rolling stock. Here an autocoach is seen undergoing major rebuilding. The substantial wood framing needs to be checked for evidence of decay.
A. C. Butcher

Left:
The framework is required to support the steel sheeting which forms the exterior surface. This is a GWR four-wheeled coach, No 975. *Great Western Society*

Right:
The interior of the vehicle is generally of more importance to the non-enthusiast visitor than the exterior shine. The GWR style of decor is evident in the restoration of this vehicle. *Great Western Society*

Above:
Hard work by volunteers on the Severn Valley Railway resulted in this superbly finished Hawksworth coach, seen here at Bewdley. *Great Western (SVR) Association*

Below:
The Railway Preservation Society of Ireland was responsible for the restoration of this LMS (NCC) coach. *C. P. Friel*

Owner Societies

This list gives details of groups or societies which own locomotives as detailed within this book. An (F) or (A) after the name indicates whether they are members of the ARPS, addresses of these societies appear on either page 90 or 91.

15xx Trust, Severn Valley, GWR 1501
51xx Fund, Severn Valley, GWR 5164
1708 Loco Pres Trust (F), Midland Railway Centre, MR 1708 and industrial
2251 Class Fund, Severn Valley GWR 3205
2857 Fund, Severn Valley, GWR 2857
4141 Fund, Severn Valley, GWR 4141
4150 Loco Fund Severn Valley, GWR 4150
4566 Fund, Severn Valley, GWR 4566
4920 Dumbleton Hall Pres Soc, Dart Valley, GWR 4920
5542 Fund, West Somerset, GWR 5542
6024 Pres Soc (A), Quainton Road, GWR 6024
6634 Loco Co, East Somerset, GWR 6634
9466 Group, Quainton Road, GWR 9466
13809 Pres Group, Midland Railway Centre, S&DJR 13809
34105 Light Pacific Group, Mid Hants, SR 34105
75014 Loco Ops Group, North Yorkshire Moors, BR 75014
75069 Fund, Severn Valley, BR 75069
76017 Standard 4 Loco Group, Mid Hants, BR 76017
80064 Loco Group, Dart Valley, BR 80064
92212 Holdings Ltd, Great Central, BR 92212
A4 Loco Soc (A), Steamtown, LNER 4498
Battle of Britain Loco Pres Soc (A), Nene Valley, SR 34081
Britannia Loco Soc (A), Nene Valley, BR 70000
Bulleid Soc Ltd (F), Bluebell, SR 30096 and 21C123
Camelot Loco Soc (A), Bluebell, BR 73082
Cotswold Diesel Pres Soc, Gloucester-Warwickshire, BR D9537
Cotswold Loco Pres Ltd, Gloucester-Warwickshire, GWR 2807
Diesel & Electric Group, West Somerset, BR D7017, D9526 and D7018 (Didcot)
Diesel Traction Group, North Yorkshire Moors, BR D821, D7029, D8568 and D1015 (Swindon)
Deltic Pres Soc, North Yorkshire Moors, BR 55.009, 55.019
Dowty Railway Pres Soc (F), Gloucester-Warwickshire, industrials
Duke of Gloucester Steam Loco Trust (A), Great Central, BR 71000
Erlestoke Manor Fund, Severn Valley, GWR 7802, 7812
Essex Loco Soc, North Yorkshire Moors, SR 841
Foremarke Hall Loco Group, Swindon & Cricklade, GWR 7903
Foxcote Manor Soc (A), Cambrian Railways, GWR 7822
Gresley Soc (A), Great Central, LNER 4744
Great Western Railway Pres Group, Swanage, GWR 6695
Great Western Steam Loco Group, Gloucester-Warwickshire, GWR 5952, 7821, 7828
Great Western (SVR) Assoc, Severn Valley, GWR 9303
H Class Trust, Bluebell, SECR 263
Highland Loco Co Ltd, Strathspey, LMS 46512
Hinton Manor Fund, Severn Valley, GWR 7819
Ivatt Loco Trust (A), Quainton Road, LMS 41298, 41313, 46447 and industrial
Ivatt 4 Fund, Severn Valley, LMS 41306
London Midland Soc, Mid Hants, LMS 44123, 47324
L&Y Saddle Tanks Fund (A), Keighley & Worth, L&Y 19, 752, 51218
Liverpool Loco Pres Group (A), Steamport, industrials
Maid Marian Loco Fund (F), Bala, industrial
Maunsell Loco Soc Ltd (A), Bluebell, SR 541, 30847, 1618
Merchant Navy Loco Press Group (F), Bulmer, SR 35028
Midland 4F Pres Soc (F), Keighley & Worth, MR 43924
Midland & Great Northern Rly Soc (F), North Norfolk, LNER 7564, 61572
Manchester Rail & Travel Soc (A), Severn Valley, LMS 47383
North Eastern Loco Pres Croup (F), North Yorkshire Moors, LNER 2005, 2238, 2392
P&O Line Soc, Gloucester-Warwickshire, SR 35006
Pannier Tank Fund, Severn Valley, GWR 5764, 7715
Passenger Tank Fund, Severn Valley, BR 80079
Princess Elizabeth Loco Soc, Bulmer LMS 6201
Scottish Loco Pres Trust Fund, Strathspey, CR 828
Scottish Loco Owners Group, Scottish RPS, BR 80105
Somerset & Dorset Museum Trust, (A), West Somerset, S&DJR 88 and industrials
Southern Electric Group (F), Nene Valley, electric stock
Southern Steam Trust (A), Swanage, BR 80078, 80104
South Yorkshire 3F Fund, Keighley & Worth, LMS 47279
Stanier 8F Loco Soc (A), Severn Valley, LMS 8233
Stanier Mogul Fund, Severn Valley, LMS 2968
Standard 4 Pres Soc, Keighley & Worth, BR 75078, 78022
Standard Nine Loco Group, North Yorkshire Moors, BR 92134
Steam Power Trust (A), Middleton, LNER 1310
Thompson B1 Loco Soc (A), Great Central, LNER 61264
Urie S15 Loco Pres Group (A), Mid Hants, LSWR 30499, 506
Wainwright C Class Pres Soc (F), Bluebell, SECR 592
Witherslack Hall Loco Soc, Great Central, GWR 6990
Y7 Loco Soc, Great Central, LNER 985

Members of the Association of Railway Preservation Societies

Full Members

Bluebell Railway Preservation Society: Mr P. Thomas, 'Grey Friars' Gravelye Lane, Haywards Heath, Sussex.

Brockham Museum Association/Brockham Museum Trust: Mr D. H. Smith, 14 Sydney Road, Haywards Heath, West Sussex RH16 1PZ

The Bulleid Society Limited: Mr R. T. Price, 3 Railway Cottages, Lywood Common, Ardingly, West Sussex

H. P. Bulmer Limited: Mr A. V. Ryder, 34 Wordsworth Road, Whitecross, Hereford HR4 0QB

Cambrian Railways Society Limited: c/o Delamere, Old Chirk Road, Gobowen, Oswestry, Salop

Chasewater Railway Society: Mr B. J. Bull, 173 Parkeston Crescent, Kingstanding, Birmingham B44 0PS

Colne Valley Railway Company Limited: Mr J. R. Hymas, Castle Hedingham Station, Yeldham Road, Castle Hedingham, Halstead, Essex CO9 3DZ

Corris Railway Society: Mr A. H. Lawson, 165 Gynsill Lane, Anstey, Leicester LE7 7AN

Darlington Railway Preservation Society: Old S&DR Goods Depot, Station Road, Hopetown, Darlington DL3 6ST

Dart Valley Railway Association: 11 Amados Drive, Merafield, Plympton, Plymouth, Devon PL7 3TS

Dean Forest Railway Society Limited: Mr C. A. Bladon, Laurel Cottage, Northwood Green, Westbury-on-Severn, Gloucestershire

Dinting Railway Centre Limited (Bahamas Locomotive Society): Mr K. J. Tait, 73 Derby Road, Heaton Moor, Stockport, Cheshire SK4 4NG

Dowty Railway Preservation Society: Mr R. H. Wales, 7 Lypiatt Street, Tivoli, Cheltenham, Gloucestershire

East Lancashire Railway Preservation Society: Mr C. P. R. Cooke, Bury Transport Museum, Castlecroft Road, Bury, Lancashire BL9 0LN

East Somerset Railway Company Limited: Mr J. Stanaway, The Railway Station, West Cranmore, Shepton Mallet, Somerset

Festiniog Railway Society Limited: Mr W. R. Holton, 42 Hanbury Road, Dorridge, Solihull, West Midlands B93 8DW

Foxfield Light Railway Society Limited: Mr B. Allen, 25 Drubbery Lane, Dresden, Stoke-on-Trent ST3 4BH

Friends of the National Railway Museum: Mr R. Rowntree, c/o The National Railway Museum, Leeman Road, York YO2 4XJ

Great Central Railway Company: Loughborough Central Station, Loughborough

Great Western Society Limited: Mr W. J. Smith, GWS, Didcot Railway Centre, Didcot, Oxon OX11 7NJ

Gwili Railway Company Limited: 51 Neath Road, Maesteg, Mid-Glamorgan CF34 9EF

H Class Trust: Mr E. R. C. Oades, 5 Senlac Way, St Leonards-on-Sea, Sussex

Irish Steam Preservation Society Limited: Mr F. C. Flewitt, 6 Waterloo Avenue, Dublin 3, Ireland

Keighley and Worth Valley Railway Preservation Society: Mr P. Eastham, Secretary, 79 Cedar Street, Skew Bridge, Blackburn, Lancs BB1 9TQ

Lakeside Railway Society: Mr I. D. Owen, 83 Camberton Road, Linslade, Leighton Buzzard, Bedfordshire LU7 7UW.

Leighton Buzzard Narrow Gauge Railway Society Limited: Mr D. F. Trevelion, Secretary, 18 Hornbeam Close, Leighton Buzzard, Bedfordshire LU7 8UX

Locomotive Club of Great Britain: Mr R. L. Patrick, 45 Millfield Lane, York YO1 3AW

Locomotive Owners Group (Scotland) Limited: Mr J. L. Stevenson, 22 Comely Bank Place, Edinburgh EH4 1DU

Maid Marian Locomotive Fund: Mr D. C. Carrington, 223 Sunnybank Road, Unsworth, Bury, Lancashire BL9 8JU

Main Line Steam Trust Limited: Mr S. L. Jacobs, Great Central Railway Station, Loughborough, Leicestershire LE11 1SS

Merchant Navy Locomotive Preservation Society Limited: Mr R. Abercrombie, 12 Inglewood Avenue, Heatherside, Camberley, Surrey

Mid-Hants Railway Trust Ltd: Mr R. Higgs, Alresford Station, Alresford, Hants SO24 9JG

Middleton Railway Trust Limited: Mrs I. Brampton, 21 Bedford Road, Wakefield WP1 2AA

Midland & Great Northern Joint Railway Society Limited: The Librarian, Sheringham Station, Sheringham, Norfolk NR26 8RA

Midland 4F Preservation Society: Mr I. Johnson, 13 Shepley Close, Hazel Grove, Stockport, Cheshire SK7 6JJ

Midland Railway Trust Limited: Mr R. Clegg, 9 Hawthorn Crescent, Findern, Derby DE6 6AN

Nene Valley International Steam Railway: Wansford Station, Stibbington, Peterborough PE8 9LR

North Eastern Locomotive Preservation Group: Mr D. A. Pennock, 88 Featherstone Road, Newton Hall, Durham DH1 5YP

North York Moors Historical Railway Trust: Mr J. R. Craven, 35 Lowdale Lane, Sleights, Whitby, Yorkshire

Plym Valley Railway Association: Mr B. Mills, 17 Birchland Avenue, Beacon Park, Plymouth PL2 3LA

Railway Preservation Society of Ireland: Mr R. Morton, 79 Sharman Road, Belfast BT9 5HE

Ravenglass and Eskdale Railway Preservation Society Limited: Mr D. Pickup, The Retreat, Ravenglass, Cumbria CA18 1SW

Redditch Steam Locomotive Preservation Society: Mr E. W. Wingrove, Plymouth Road, Southcrest, Redditch, Worcestershire B97 4DP

Ruislip Lido Railway Society: Mr D. L. Parker, 8 Brendon Gardens, South Harrow, Middlesex

Scottish Railway Preservation Society: Dr A. Glen, 21 Monks Road, Airdrie, Lanarkshire ML6 2QW.

Severn Valley Railway Company Limited: Mr M. J. Draper, 'Wynniatts', The Hill, Abberley, Worcester WR6 6BZ

Sittingbourne & Kemsley Light Railway Limited: Mr M. Burton, 85 Balmoral Avenue, Gillingham, Kent

Stanier 8F Locomotive Society Limited: Mr W. Murray, Dusthouse Cottage, Dusthouse Lane, Tardebigge, Bromsgrove, Worcestershire

Steam in Hereford Limited (6000 Locomotive Association): Mr E. T. Taylor, 18 Merestone Road, Redhill, Hereford HR2 7PS

Stour Valley Railway Preservation Society: Mr L. Houghton, Secretary, Old Railway Tavern, Station Road, Wakes Colne, Colchester, Essex CO6 2DS

Southern Electric Group: Mr A. C. Holmewood, 48 Church Lane, Chessington, Surrey KT9 2DW

Telford Horsehay Steam Trust: Mr R. I. Stanley, 173 Sundorne Road, Shrewsbury, Shropshire SY1 4RN

Tenterden Railway Company Limited (Kent & East Sussex Railway): The Company Secretary, Tenterden Railway Company Limited, Tenterden Town Station, Tenterden, Kent TN30 6HE

Vintage Carriages Trust: Mr C. G. Smyth, 26 Cambridge Road, Crosby, Leicester

Wainwright 'C' Preservation Society: Mr I. Demaid, 69 Bromley Gardens, Bromley, Kent BR2 0ES

Welshpool and Llanfair Light Railway Preservation Company Limited: Mr M. A. Elliot, 22 Speedwell Drive, Heswell L60 2SZ

Wight Locomotive Society: The Secretary, Railway Station, Haven Street, Ryde, Isle of Wight PO33 4DS

Worcester Locomotive Society: Mr D. R. G. Nowell, 1 Ranelagh Street, Hereford

Yorkshire Dales Railway Museum Trust: J. M. Whitney, 8 Aspin Way, Knaresborough, North Yorks HG5 8HL

275 Railway Squadron RCT (V): Major G. Goodman, 4 Maple Close, Alresford, Hants

1247 Society: Capt W. G. Smith, Bartley Barnes Farm, Grafton Regis, Towcester NN12 7SS

1708 Locomotive Preservation Trust Limited: Mr G. S. Mimms, 19 St Mary's Park, Nailsea, Bristol BS19 2RW

6201 Princess Elizabeth Society Limited: Mr E. Whitlock, 7 Cherry Walk, Lydney, Glos. Tel: Lydney 8026

Associate Members

Avonside Steam Preservation Society: Mr K. Rodgers, 58 Castle Street, Cambridge CB3 0AP

A4 Locomotive Society Limited: Mr G. R. Pope, Secretary, 25 Acacia Road, St Johns Wood, London

Battle of Britain Locomotive Preservation Society: Mr R. J. Tanner, 157 Harrowden Road, Bedford MK42 0RM

Bitton Railway Company Limited: Mr G. Clark, 12 Cramwell Grove, Whitchurch, Bristol BS14 9QR

Bowes Railway Company Limited: Mr G. F. Mountford, 27 Glencoe Avenue, Southfield Green, Cramlington NE23 6EH

Brechin Railway Preservation Society: The Station, 2 Park Road, Brechin, Angus, Scotland

Brecon Mountain Railway Association: Mr R. Nurdin, 28 Clwyd, North Cliff, Penarth CF6 1DZ

Bressingham Steam Engine Trust: Mr A. Bloom, Bressingham Hall, Bressingham, Diss, Norfolk IP22 2AB

Britannia Locomotive Society: Mr A. R. Lawson, 14 Calluna Drive, Bletchley, Milton Keynes MK3 6QL

Cadeby Light Railway: Rev E. R. Boston, Cadeby Rectory, Cadeby, Hinckley, Nuneaton, Warwickshire

Caerphilly Railway Society Limited: Mr A. Smith, 51 Worcester Crescent, Newport, Gwent

Camelot Locomotive Society: Mr P. W. Gibbs, 71 Broadstone Road, Harpenden, Hertfordshire AL5 1RE

Conwy Valley Railway Museum Limited: c/o Burtons of Walsall Ltd, 65 Bradford Street, Walsall, West Midlands DL3 6ST

Cheltenham & Stratford Railway: Mr S. W. Branchett, 'Marlborough', Blenheim Drive, Bredon, Tewksbury, Gloucestershire GL20 7NQ

Cornish Steam Locomotive Preservation Society Ltd: Mr M. Orme, 3 Jubilee Terrace, Goonhavern, Truro, Cornwall TR4 9JY

Cotswold Steam Preservation Limited: Mr J. M. Colley, 387 Hurcott Road, Kidderminster, Worcestershire

Dyfed Railway Company Limited: Miss E. Perry, Bwlch Cae Brith, Cafel Iwan Road, Newcastle-Emlyn, Dyfed

Eastleigh Railway Preservation Society: Mr J. W. Gregory, Civic Offices, Leigh Road, Eastleigh, Hants SO5 4YN

Forest Pannier Tank Fund: Mr J. S. Metherall, 15 Sudbrook Way, Gloucester

Forest Prairie Fund: Mr D. G. Phelps, Upper Sandaway, Hangerberry, Lydbrook, Gloucester

Foxcote Manor Society: Mr B. Ellery, 11 Lightfoot Street, Chester CH2 3AH

Gravesend Railway Enthusiasts Society: Mr I. G. Rushforth, 74 Main Road, Longfield, Dartford, Kent

Great Western Preservations Limited: Mr A. R. Machon, 15 Calder Close, Maidenhead, Berks SL6 7RS

Great Central Railway Coach Group: Mr J. S. Parsons, 8 Grendon Way, Bierton, Aylesbury, Bucks HP22 5DD

The Gresley Society: Mr P. Holmes, Argyll Cottage, Thurgarton Quarters, Oxton Road, Southwell, Notts NG25 0RW

GWR 813 Preservation Fund: Mr P. Goss, 23 Hatchmere, Thornbury, Bristol BS12 2EU

Hexham Rolling Stock Group: Mr G. Hall, 24 Welton Close, Stocksfield, Northumberland NE43 7EP

Hull and Barnsley Railway Stock Fund: Mr A. Halman, 6 Chequerfield Court, Chequerfield Avenue, Pontefract, West Yorks WP8 2TQ

Ivatt Locomotive Trust: Mr R. B. Miller, 'Ducal', 25 Loudham Road, Little Chalfont, Amersham, Buckinghamshire

Lambton No 29 Syndicate: Mr J. M. Richardson, c/o Midland Bank Limited, 1 Murray Street, Filey, North Yorkshire YO14 9DB

Lancashire & Yorkshire Saddletanks Fund: Mr R. S. Greenwood, 8 Oxford Avenue, Rochdale, Lancashire

Leicester Industrial Locomotive Group: Mr J. P. Bailey, 414 Hinckley Road, Leicester LE3 0WA

Liverpool Locomotive Preservation Group: Mr K. Soper, 86 Moorland Road, Maghull, Liverpool L31 5JW

Llangollen Railway Society: Mr A. Terry, 33 Deeside, Ellesmere Port, S. Wirral, Cheshire

Lloyds Railway Society: Mr P. E. Wood, 33 Beechwood Road, Caterham, Surrey CR3 6NA

LM 2MT 46464 Trust: Mr I. N. Fraser, Palace Gates, Viewfield Road, Arbroath, Angus DD11 2BS

London & North Western Society: Mr J. C. James, 'Solaby', 4 Longview Drive, Huyton, Liverpool L36 6EE

Lord Fisher Locomotive Group: Mr B. G. Buckfield, Newton Gardens, Park Road, Paulton, Bristol BS18 5NF

Manchester Rail Travel Society: Mr F. G. Cronin, 12 Chiltern Road, Ramsbottom, Lancashire

Manston Locomotive Preservation Society: Mr J. Wickham, 76 Southwood Road, Ramsgate, Kent CT11 0AL

Maunsell Locomotive Society: 7 West Point, Newick, Lewes, East Sussex BN8 4NU

North Eastern Railway Coach Group: Mr P. J. Brumby, 48 Laburnum Walk, Gilberdyke, Brough, Humberside HU15 2TU

North Staffordshire Railway Society: Mr L. M. Budden, Chedleton Station, Chedleton, Staffordshire ST13 7EE

Peak Rail Operations Limited: Mr S. R. Broadbent, 53 Lower Market Road, Broadbottom, Hyde, Cheshire SK4 6AA

Peak Railway Society Ltd: Mr D. G. Adams, Ivy Cottage, Dam Lane, Riveton, Warrington WA3 6LG

Pontypool & Blaenavon Railway Society: Ms L. Shiach, Woodland Cottage, Penygarn Road, Pontypool, Gwent

Quainton Railway Society Limited: Mr R. B. Miller, 'Ducal', 25 Loudham Road, Little Chalfont, Amersham, Bucks

Railway Vehicle Preservations: Mr D. Pearce, 77 Gosling House, Sutton Street, Shadwell, London E1

Rheilffordd Llyn Tegid Limited (Bala Lake Railway): Mr G. H. Barnes, General Manager, 'Yr Orsaf', Llanuwchllyn, Bala, Gwynedd

Romney, Hythe & Dymchurch Railway Association: Mr M. Neighbour, 67 Ailsa Avenue, St Margarets, Twickenham TW1 1NF

Salisbury Steam Locomotive Preservation Trust: Mr E. J. Roper, 33 Victoria Road, Wilton, Salisbury, Wiltshire SP2 0OZ

Shackerstone Railway Society Limited: Mr A. G. Briggs, 40 Newstead Avenue, Burbage, Hinckley

Somerset & Dorset Railway Trust: Mr R. Kite, 'The Poplars', Theale, Wedmore, Somerset BS28 4SN

Southern Steam Trust: Mr M. D. Stone, Southern Steam Trust, The Station, Swanage, Dorset

South Tynedale Railway Preservation Society: Mr S. Dyke, 11 Norley Avenue, Sunderland SR5 1JY

South Western Circle: Mr T. R. Page, 21 Cowley Crescent, Walton-on-Thames, Surrey KT12 5RH

South Yorkshire Railway Preservation Society: Mr D. Lawson, 100 Ellerton Road, Frith Park, Sheffield S5 6UG

Stanier Black Five Locomotive Preservation Society: Mr D. J. Porter, 29 High Street, Shoreham, Kent

Steamport Southport: Mr C. Forest, 14 Franklands, Longton, Preston, Lancashire

Steam Power Trust '65: Mr K. H. Cockerill, 30 Hartburn Lane, Stockton-on-Tees TS18 3QH

Strathspey Railway Association: Mr R. Black, 37 Castle Avenue, Balloch, Alexandria, Dunbartonshire G83 8HU

Swindon & Cricklade Railway Society: Mrs R. M. Palk, 5 Bradene Close, Wootton Bassett, Swindon, Wilts SN4 8DG

Talyllyn Railway Company: Wharf Station, Tywyn, Gwynedd LL36 9EY

Thompson B1 Locomotive Society: Mr J. G. Gwnett, 11 Valance End, Dunstable LU6 3LR

Urie S15 Preservation Group: Mr T. Ball, 'Alice Cottage', 31 Sydney Road, Walton-on-Thames KT12 2N4

Welsh Industrial and Maritime Museum: Dr E. S. Owen-Jones, Welsh Industrial & Maritime Museum, Bute Street, Docks, Cardiff CF1 6AN

West Somerset Railway Company: The Railway Station, Minehead, Somerset

Winchcombe Railway Museum Association: Mr T. R. Petchey, 23 Gloucester Street, Winchcombe, Glos

1857 Society: Mr K. R. Bowen, 18 Lochmore Close, Hollycroft, Hinckley, Leics

6024 Preservation Society Limited: Mr C. D. Abbot-Stone, 68 Ashbourne Parade, Hanger Lane, Ealing, London W5 3QS

9642 Preservation Group: Mr W. T. Jones, 'Bryn Awelon', 55 Salisbury Road, Maesteg, Glamorgan CF34 9EH

45428 Stanier Class Five Locomotive Society Limited: Mr J. B. Hollingsworth, 'Creua', Llanfrothen, Penrhyndeudraeth, Gwynedd LL48 6SH

71000 Duke of Gloucester Steam Locomotive Trust Ltd: Mr M. D. Johnson, 29 Frensham, Crown Wood, Bracknell, Berks RG12 3TQ

Late Information

New acquisitions

GWR No 3802 for Plym Valley Railway
GWR No 3803 for Dart Valley Railway
GWR No 3850 for West Somerset Railway
GWR No 4953 for Dean Forest Railway
GWR No 7229 for Plym Valley Railway
LMS No 45337 for Bury Transport Museum
SR No 34072 for Swindon & Cricklade Railway
SR No 34073 for Brighton Locomotive Works
BR No 40.106 for Great Central Railway
BR No 40.145 for Bury Transport Museum
BR No 55.015 for Midland Railway Centre
SAR Garrett No 2352 for Greater Manchester Museum of Science and Industry

Transfers

BR No 80064 to Bluebell Railway

Back cover:
No 34092 *City of Wells* heads towards Haworth at Mytholmes with a service from Oxenhope, 11 July 1982. *B. Dobbs*

Association of Railway Preservation Societies Ltd

Company Limited by Guarantee and not having a share capital.
Registered in England No 1222717

(Registered Office: 21 Market Place, Wednesbury, West Midlands WS10 7AY)

Directors/Council of Management

Chairman
Captain Peter F. Manisty, MBE, RN (Retd), 2 Cleaver Square, Kennington, London SE11 4DW. Tel: 01-735 5012

General Secretary
Mr D. P. Madden, The Station Sheringham, Norfolk NR26 8RA. Tel: 0263-822045

Treasurer
Mr R. T. Yates, FCA, 21 Market Place, Wednesbury, West Midlands, WS10 7AY

Membership Secretary
Mr E. V. Boxell, 17 Azalea Close, Uxbridge Road, Hanwell, London W7 3QA. Tel: 01-840 2917

Meetings Officer
Mr P. Overstone, 33 Palmerston Place, Edinburgh EH12 5AU

Legal Officer and Vice Chairman
Mr D. Morgan, 7 Cheyne Place, London SW3 4HH

Publicity Officer
Mr John Morfin, 150 Southcoates Lane, Hull HU9 3AJ. Tel: 0482-705 315

Publicity Assistant
Mr J. C. Jeffery, 'Failte', 15 Hemmingford Crescent, Stanground, Peterborough PE2 8LL

Journal Editor
Rev E. J. Buck, 40 Chapel Lane, Wymondham, Norfolk NR18 0DL. Tel: Wymondham (0953) 602153

Mr P. G. Ransom, 'Woodside', Craggon, Lochearnhead, Perthshire FK19 8QD

Mr Brian Armitage, 15 Stoneham Close, Petersfield, Hants GU32 3BX. Tel: 0703 67586

Mr C. Smyth, 26 Cambridge Road, Crosby, Leicester LE5 5SH

All general correspondence and enquiries should be addressed to the: General Secretary, ARPS, Sheringham station, Norfolk NR26 8RA, England. Tel: 0263-822045

Private Membership Application Form (1984)

To a person actively interested in nationwide railway preservation as opposed to one particular preservation scheme, PRIVATE MEMBERSHIP of the ASSOCIATION OF RAILWAY PRESERVATION SOCIETIES LTD can offer many advantages. Three major meetings are organised annually, often at the railway site of a leading Full Member Society. Here one can meet well known personalities in the railway preservation world, and the host society invariably lays on a full day's programme which is both stimulating and enjoyable.

The ARPS Journal is sent to members, containing mostly the latest news of member societies' activities but also full of interesting titbits such as lists of steam locomotives for sale.

Railways Restored and other publications by Ian Allan in conjunction with ARPS are made available at reduced prices.

To: Mr E. V. Boxell, 17 Azalea Close, Uxbridge Road, Hanwell, London W7 3QA

Name ....
(BLOCK LETTERS PLEASE)

Address ....

....

Post Code .... Telephone ....

Subscription enclosed .... Donation enclosed ....

Private membership costs £6 per year (1 April-31 March); £7 (1 January-31 March 1985) (15 months). Life membership £60.

57436
54464

34042

Index